Lights

zine: issue number one

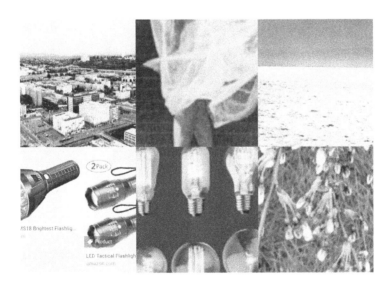

PLEASURE BOAT STUDIO: A NONPROFIT LITERARY PRESS

PLEASUREBOATSTUDIO.COM

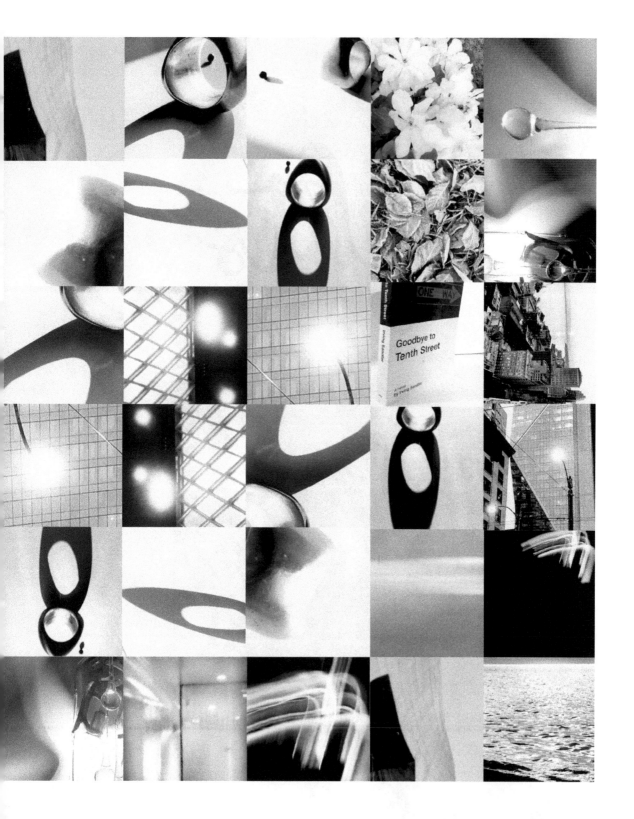

ISBN 978-0-912887-96-8
Produced and designed by Lauren Grosskopf , Publisher
Lauren@pleasureboatstudio.com

Pleasure Boat Studio books are available
through your favorite bookstore and through the following:
PLEASURE BOAT STUDIO: A LITERARY PRESS
pleasureboatstudio.com | Seattle, Washington
& Baker & Taylor, Ingram, Amazon.com & Barnesandnoble.com

NOTE: Prior to 2017 when Jack Estes retired Pleasure Boat Studio to Lauren Grosskopf,
he published unique books for 20 years, 15 of which were in NY, NY. Jack Estes
is still on the Board and remains the main editor for Pleasure Boat books.

LIGHTS zine is a creative space for a variety of local and Pleasure Boat Studio talents, and this pandemic-quarantine is a fertile time for creative-connection.

THE IMPETUS began with the discovery of John Christopher Nelson's short stories while working the shelves at Trader Joes—where I worked a couple of years ago along with many other creative, friendly folks, to help pay the bills while pursuing publishing and motherhood. I enjoyed his stories a lot, and I wished I could publish them, but knew it wasn't possible. I also began feeling sorry about saying no to a few great poets...again having neither the extra time, nor recourses to help share their work with people who might appreciate it. The zine seemed a great solution and was bolstered by the desire to gain more exposure for Pleasure Boat Studio in Seattle, and perhaps beyond, in a fun way.

BEHIND THE NAME: When first coming up with the name for this collective way to publish more people, I was thinking of one word possibilities, starting with boat related ideas to pair the theme with 'Pleasure Boat': mast, anchor, waves, skiff, oar, etc.

Then, 'lights' came to me, simple as that and I liked it and stuck with it. The feeling of it felt warm, infinite, fresh, mysterious, clean, airy, mystical, soft, glowing, urban, can't even describe it really.... Then, I got to thinking of forms of light, natural and electric and the feeling and meanings "Light" can evoke by what light is cast, by which angle and direction, and what lights can show or reveal, reflect or bare witness to. Lights illuminate the dark so we can see, so we can see where we're going, and see where we are.

So, take a glimpse and a ponder into what these contributors want to show you, for what they may put a spotlight on in our lit up world, however dark it might get sometimes.

Lauren Grosskopf, Publisher & Designer,
Pleasure Boat Studio

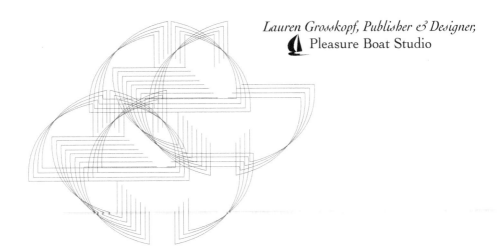

SHIN YU PAI

Sangha
Imprints
Shamanic
The Century Building
All Beings Our Teachers

Sangha

of the three jewels
the most precious
is the community

of practitioners, I feel
this truth acutely when
I conjoin with another

disciple & we pivot to bow
in unison to the circle, as we
retire from sacred space

honoring how you & I once
turned towards a roomful of friends,
raised our hands to our hearts

humbling ourselves, to ourselves
bowing with you, not to you
the gaze turning downwards

my heart opened, giving
silent gratitude too
for who we were then

I M P R I N T S

at the urban science museum
baby ducks fall into step

around us, as our bodies
cast shadows across pavement,

you invoke the fantasia of Disney
as I brood over a more naked truth

we must not pet the wildlife
such a fine line between

helping and harming

imprint of mother, imprint
of lover what it felt like to be held

in loving tenderness & its inverse
—the rough touch of predator,

tearing the feathers out one
at a time, we learn the habits

of want at a young age,
the harm to self,

a script I choose
to now unwrite

shamanic

when I hold the bronze
mold in my palm, I see

the likeness of a menstrual cup,
it's been a long spell since

I spoke to those ancestors

lately, giving them the cold
shoulder for sending me chaos

disguised as a lover who called me
witch when his body erupted

in shingles for his own betrayals,
it was medicine I asked for,

when I invoked them in
the old-growth forest, now

as I turn over the act of casting
108 miniature chortens, I think of

what makes a gesture divine
to choose between Murphy's

soap and olive oil as standard
mold release, shoving a capsule

of ibuprofen into the clay body
or offering leaves of sage

what makes anything magic

THE CENTURY BUILDING

in a silent bid to protect itself against
historic designation, the property

owners of 10 Harrison Street remove
the mid-century sun panels obscuring

office windows to alter the appearance
of Bystrom & Grecoof's post-stressed

concrete and brutalism
Pacific Northwest minimalism

made less to achieve a fuller market value
defensible as needed seismic improvement

the variance between a $3-4M swing
in sales price, board members raised

their hands to discuss stewardship,
fiduciary duty of an organization's

stakeholders – trading on imaginary
"children" – the real estate developer argued

"you can always build a building,
but you can't fulfill a kid's dream"

how a pass-through funder touches
the lives of disadvantaged youth

at a far distance, an abstract audience
easier still to picture than the Queen Anne

Historic Society – corporate types skirt
a motion to apply stucco atop brick exterior

to change a street-facing façade
further impairing landmark status

the occupants deafened by jackhammers

all beings, our teachers

the jazz poet invited me to lunch
on the premise of electing me
for a poetry prize, when I arrived

for our meeting he opened the door
in his bathrobe, his apartment staged
with Orientalist porn

the AAPI novelist recruited me to teach
without pay —I looked the right part
to a group of Pinay teens

she'd later take to Manila
as research subjects; when I
explained I needed work that paid

the rent she said I failed
in my responsibilities

the mentor handed me a news clipping
from *The NY Times* —
here I am giving you a poem

the piece was on Vietnamese
tonal language speakers
Why we have perfect pitch

I stopped learning Mandarin by the time I was 8

Now I am older, when I bump
into former instructors outside
of the classroom they say

She was my student.
She studied with me.
I taught her.

For many years my best
teachers were books, they
would not force me with

callused ashen hands, no
way of being misread
this aversion to learning

to teaching sometimes I miss
sharing my mind with others
in these moments I turn

to you and say claim this
beauty that belongs to you
and make it yours

ENSŌ
SHIN YU PAI

visit **shinyupai.com**
for more on
books,
publications,
events
& book art

to read and order her new release:
Ensō from entreriosbooks.com

Lyric World: Conversations with Contemporary Poets.
In collaboration with Town Hall, Shin Yu Pai
began producing a poetry series in January 2020.
The series seeks to explore the social role of poetry,
as it gives voice and attention to the human experience.
Streamable: https://www.kuow.org/stories/a-world-where-
poetry-meets-magic-and-wonder

A contributor as well to
Make It True Meets Medusario

This poem from Beautiful Passing Lives *by Edward Harkness
was chosen as a dedication for all those who, enmasse,
too abruptly lost, are losing, or will lose their lives
and/or their loved ones lives due to the Covid-19 Corona viru;*

*to all those grieving lost ones,
regardless the reason their passing;*

*to my mother who lost her life to cancer when I was fifteen,
to my grandparents who survived the Holocaust, and to our
family that didn't, and to everyone else along the way...*

I guess one could say: to everyone ever.

Beautiful Passing Lives

When our beach fire had died,
the last embers dimming like stars
and waves clapped and hissed,
quieter on the out tide,

sometime after midnight
we saw on the black horizon
lights of a passenger ship
some five miles off shore,

glide on nothing. No moon.
All those lives, we thought,
those beautiful passing lives.
We must have watched

for an hour the slow constellation
head north, hidden for a time
behind a sea stack, then glittering again
like a better world,

the one we believed would arrive
one day, still on its journey, perhaps,
making only brief appearances,
as comets do, reminding us

of something out there
that may never strike land,
but glitter still, and glide
off shore on nothing.

Beautiful Passing Lives
Holding the New Baby, I Feel
the Feather Weight of My Death
To the Woman at the March

Holding the New Baby, I Feel
the Feather Weight of My Death

He has arrived earlier than expected,
light as a small bag of apples
in my lap. Now and then he rouses
to blink the black opals of his eyes,
still mostly sightless after all that time
in the dark. I'm his father's father and —
oh, what the hell — I'm on a short leash,
wondering if my departure will likewise
be earlier than expected — which is,
I suppose, always the case. The future
announces itself as a quiet, insistent
tap at the door. The new being
in the crook of my arm yawns.
Now his lips part in a reflexive dream smile
I take to mean he finds the condition
of being alive curious, wryly amusing,
as if to say, *So, where am I exactly?*
on this bright November morning,
a day I've already subtracted
from the dwindling total. His eyelids flutter,
thinner than the skin of a hatchling robin.
Now I'm reminded babies must eat.
His mother whisks him out of my arms,
off to a rocker in a dark corner,
where, after a few urgent squalls, he's quiet,

16

the sucking audible even from across
the room. I'm empty-handed once more,
happy in a way I've never been.
I plan to attend his third birthday,
already scripting, after the other kids
have left with their frosting-smeared chins,
the conversation we might have,
the one where I tell him I held him
when he was one day old, his eyes
were exquisite blueberries, different
than the gray-green they are now.
He'll be only mildly impressed,
more interested instead in tearing off
the paper of one last gift:
a box with a silver latch and key.
He's wide-eyed to lift the wooden lid,
to get a glimpse of things to come.
I'm more intrigued in learning how
to tie together strings of time,
quilting swatches of months and years,
stitching my life to his, as if I had such power,
the slightest ability to forestall for even
an instant that insistent tap
from arriving sooner than expected.
Still, I'm swaddled in the glory
of the moment, thankful to have held him,
to listen to his mother hum in the dark,
to hear the creak of the rocker
on the hardwood floor.

~Cosmo MacKenzie Harkness,
b. November 5, 2019

To the Woman at the March

She was frail, bespectacled, in a dated
but flowery housedress, light
for the warmth of the day. Her hat,
too, seemed to come from another era,

likewise bedecked with flowers —
small, needle-pointed rosebuds, I believe
they were. Me, white. She, black.
We had marched together with the others,

some thousands, neither of us speaking,
turning now and then to smile as if
to acknowledge that we were, both of us,
alone, thrown together by chance,

hemmed by the river of our fellows
flowing salmon-like to the rhythm of someone
drumming, someone playing a recorder,
another far ahead exhorting us

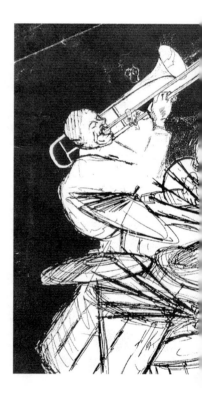

with a bullhorn to chant in unison
our anger, our conviction — The people,
united, will never be defeated.
The march ended at a park where,

more or less unscripted, our throng formed
a great choir before the makeshift stage,

to await the dozen speakers gathered
with their prepared sermons.
Somewhere from behind rose
the hymn "We Shall Overcome."
That's when, without looking, she took
my hand, squeezed it not gently,

and joined in. I felt her bright contralto
first as a hum, so pure it frightened me,
its current rising through my wrist,
up my arm, where it settled in my chest.

And I, who cannot carry a tune to save
my life, sang Oh, deep in my heart,
I do believe, we shall overcome some day,
wishing as I sang never to let go.

© N.J. PEACOCK '91

ART *by Seattle fine artist*
NANCY PEACOCK
*You can see more of her work at KUOW
where she has 30 pieces on permenant exhibit.*

THE EVERY DAY

SARAH PLIMPTON

SURFACE

I stumbled

from the height

and fell

against the sky

broken from the edge

the cliff

black against

the stars

falling from underneath

the ground had

disappeared

THE OTHER SUN

a sudden light

but then you had already gone

the eye is so straight

looking behind

a door to shut

and open

I had forgotten to ask

looking only once

the whole sky

was there

that bright blue

as if painted in

the other sun

THE EVERY DAY

twisted into the sky

with your hands

I'd never seen that blue before

wrung out with

the paper walls

of air

until the rain

soaked through

a smaller patch behind the grey

I'd remember once

and then again

like the sun

the every day

SARAH PLIMPTON

poems from **The Every Day**
Surface
The Other Sun
The Every Day
Edges

EDGES

an eye of broken glass

the sky on its edge

at the top of the wall

the bright line of the day

splintered

from the sun

and already dark.

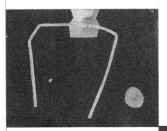

SARAH PLIMPTON is a poet and artist working in several media, including oil painting, printmaking, and artists' books. Her artwork is in such public collections as the New York Public Library and the Metropolitan Museum of Art.

Artisticly abstract in both her art and writings. Particularly captivating poems that collage into one another, with central, repeating themes/words, strung together like a folding accordion with the themes interplaying through variations of context and structure, to derive at whole new meanings, metaphors and moments, in a condensed form.

THE NOISE OF THE RAIN: The Every Day & Newer Poems, Drawings & Illustrations (Sheep Meadow Press)
https://brooklynrail.org/2017/02/books/The-Noise-of-the-Rain

PHOTOGRAPHY BY
TRAVIS WINN | TRAVISWINNPHOTO.COM
designer, artist, music producer | Joshua Tree/L.A.

COLLABORATION came about natually wandering in the
desert with travelers from Russia, coming upon an abandoned structure with a long role of tape. Fashion shows &
ceremonies coordinator / a musician:
INSTAGRAM TAGS: **katrin_raduga / InterTopol**

JOHN CHRISTOPHER NELSON

SOLA FIDE

SHORT STORY FICTION

ORIGINAL PUBLICATION: ABLE MUSE: A REVIEW OF POETRY, PROSE & ART
PRINT EDITION #21 - SUMMER 2016 / EDITED BY ALEXANDER PEPPLE
ISBN 978-1-927409-78-7 / DIGITAL ISBN 978-1-927409-79-4 / ABLEMUSE.COM

JACQUI GAUGHAN HAD A VALID—though, she felt, inexcusable—reason for being late to the prom. The unforeseen limousine fire didn't make her feel any better about missing everything that had happened prior to her arrival. Nor did the lateness of the others in her party make her own lateness any more bearable. Once she entered the gymnasium and spotted Howard Brandt and heard Madonna—the guy she'd been waiting all day to see and the song she'd been hoping all day to hear—everyone else in her group ceased to matter.

After dancing with Howard, Jacqui would find out:

1. "Footloose" was the second song to play—it was within the first three to play at last year's prom, homecoming, and winter formal. Jacqui wondered how many more formals would endure Kenny Loggins' onslaught;

2. Donny Styles pregamed too hard by himself in his stepmom's basement and was already passed out in the back of a pickup in the parking lot, ruining the tux he borrowed from his uncle Todd;

3. Tailor Rinks left the dance abruptly when her younger, prettier sister, Leslie—most people supposed they were only half-related—told Tailor she looked fat in her dress. Leslie had been drinking. Tailor had not.

But before she learned any of this, Jacqui's only concern was seeing Howard, catching his eye before he and his date left to fool around. Jacqui was sure that if Howard and Suzie Cramer hadn't already had sex, Suzie would put out tonight.

By the time Jacqui arrived, she was already upset about the electric-blue dress she was wearing. The dress did not look bad on her. She looked better than many of the girls in attendance, who had all seemingly embraced the current anti-coke trend and put on a ton of weight in the last year. Jacqui still did coke here and there. She used the word "recreational" and didn't feel it had anything to do with her not putting on weight. But for Jacqui it didn't matter that she looked better, it was that the other girls—not just at Valhalla, but at every other high school in San Diego, California, perhaps the nation—were wearing carnation-pink dresses tonight. That's what was hip this year, this season, this moment in 1985. So far tonight, Jacqui felt tragically unhip.

Three weeks later, reviewing the photos taken before the dance, Jacqui neglected to comment on her date and simply conceded to herself, "You look like Donna Lea. Christ." Earlier that year, Jacqui pierced her right ear a second and third time to mimic her friend Donna Lea and, in response to her efforts, earned no praise from her supposed friend but instead the scolds of her own father for being "less than trailer trash." Yes, for the piercings. Ear piercings.

But this feeling of tragic unhipness only lasted during the few moments between her arrival and when her song started to play. "Crazy For You" was already popular that year, but was nothing particularly special to anyone but Jacqui, who had already based her night's imagined success on whether or not the song would play.

Her date, Kenneth Kauffman, was not her first choice. Jacqui had recently left Bob Garber and her brothers had suggested Kenneth for a date. He was not ugly, but handsome was not a word anyone would use. He was too nice for her. Especially after Bob. Bob, who had already graduated. Bob, who sold drugs,

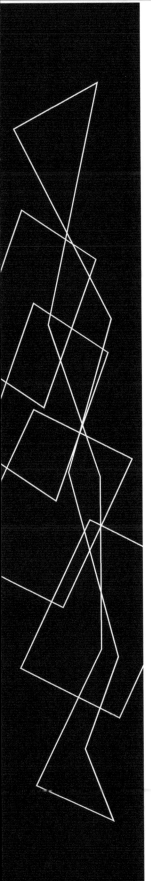

who explained away rogue panties discovered in his apartment. Someone gentlemanly like Kenneth felt foreign, unpleasant.

Her older brothers were among the first two classes to graduate from Valhalla in 1976 and 1977. The school had been erected to endure the overflow from other El Cajon high schools, which were unable to accommodate the region's exploding population. Kenneth was in Jacqui's class and his older brother was a friend of her brothers. Jacqui and Kenneth would share the Valhalla class of 1985 stamp on their diplomas, but little else besides that.

• • • • •

Mary and Maria Pernicano and Donna Lea and their dates went to dinner at Tom Ham's Lighthouse. Kenneth and his friends Marcus Szinski and Bud Lauftner had chosen something more modest for Jacqui, Tammy Strellic, and Amy Anderson: Fletcher Bowl.

The menu was not quite as extensive as the one Tom Ham offered. Fletcher Bowl had the standard bowling alley fare of hotdogs, hamburgers, fries, and pitchers of beer, the last of which the kids weren't old enough to order. But this wouldn't interfere with Jacqui's thigh-bound flask of Southern Comfort—which she wouldn't ever be able to stomach again after the summer of 1988. As for the flask, it was not comfortable, nor was it the least bit subtle. But Jacqui felt it was cool, mature. She imagined Howard would appreciate it, if he were to touch her leg and discover the flask. He would smile at her knowingly, maybe even wink.

Walking into Fletcher Bowl made the imminent disappointment of their dinner more tolerable. Just after the initial six notes of "Everybody Wants to Rule the World," the teens pushed through the doors and made their way toward the café in the back corner of the bowling alley, the song's guitar riff leading their way from the stereo speakers hanging off the walls above the casino-style carpet.

As for Jacqui's date, Kenneth would eventually become handsome enough. Nobody remarkable, but decent, better than Jacqui would give him credit for. He would end up marrying someone more attractive than him—more attractive than Jacqui. For now, that didn't matter. They were at a bowling alley. And Jacqui was about to eat a plain cheeseburger ("I'm fine without fries,") while Donna Lea was probably feasting on swordfish or piling in paella. In fact, Donna Lea was enjoying bouillabaisse, which Jacqui had never heard of and would never see on a menu.

Back to Kenneth. Sometimes youth is easier for everyone if braces are imagined as invisible. Weighing braces too heavily in high school dating decisions rules out many otherwise qualified candidates. But they are just so unavoidable. As Jacqui's tongue and teeth took in the vast array of texture and flavor offered by the complexities of Fletcher Bowl's head chef Ricky Chavez's burger, she watched Kenneth eating his. He was not careful to keep his lips closed and, even within her passing glances, Jacqui could see burger debris clotted into the wedges of the metal wires surrounding his teeth. Also, he had small hands. He was not shorter than her but not taller either, with eyes dark enough to be mysterious to high school girls but not dark enough to cause genuine intrigue. His hair had just enough of a curl to suggest a Jewish mother or father—maybe both—but Jacqui didn't care that much.

Just as Jacqui was imagining sitting across from Howard, some place nicer than this, Kenneth leaned in too close, bringing a series of chin blemishes into view. "Are you excited to dance later?"

Jacqui nodded a curt, impassive, "Yes," before slipping off to the bathroom.

She stood in the mirror and judged her dress again. Jacqui frowned at her hips as she pulled the dress down. It was too early in the night for it to be riding up. But the dress was too tight and her hips were too big. And her too-small breasts looked even smaller, pulled taut against her chest. Jacqui set the flask she'd removed from her garter on the counter and scooped her hand into the corset top to pull her breasts up into the spotlight. Jacqui was certain the sex she'd had with Bob would not be beat by Kenneth, not even met. Still, she was feeling gamesome, even if unsure whether she would allow Kenneth to kiss her.

Semi-satisfied with her reflection, despite her dress color, Jacqui pulled another swallow from her flask. There were still three shot-sized bottles nestled in the bottom of her purse. She emptied one into the flask, before throwing the bottle away. She planned to top off the flask again before entering the dance.

· · · · ·

Years later, in 1992, this was the part of the night that stood out most. There wasn't anything all that remarkable about the moment, but sitting in her hospital bed, Jacqui would catch a flash of herself behind her eyelids. Electric-blue dress, messed beach hairdo, and a chrome flask, all of them reflecting bathroom mirror light. The memory, the image, was colored by a haze not of nostalgia, but as if the memory had been recorded with eighties-quality cameras and film.

At twenty-five Jacqui would be diagnosed with undifferentiated, high-grade sarcoma, an extremely rare form of cancer that manifested as a large grapefruit, or small-sized melon, depending on who told the story, on the outside of the thigh on which she'd worn her flask seven years earlier.

The cancer was as aggressive as it was rare. The treatment was equally aggressive and Jacqui lost all of her hair and dropped from one hundred and nineteen pounds to ninety-seven. Her doctors were certain she would die and told her as politely as they could manage that she might consider saying good-byes, resolving conflicts, maybe checking some things off her list. Jacqui stared at the hospital wall. She had no idea what to do first. She had already performed her life's most brazen act seven years earlier.

Her mother was also in the room and chose to ignore the doctors, deciding her parental intuition outweighed their education and practice. And, by a complete fluke, her mother was right. Jacqui survived.

Back in 1985, this did nothing for Jacqui. No, tonight, prom night, Jacqui would return from the bathroom, having rinsed her mouth in the sink and relipsticked, adjusted her breasts one last time, to see that everyone else was finished eating and the bill was paid—she guessed Kenneth had paid for her, but did not thank him.

Although the group had arrived at the bowling alley in Kenneth's parents' van, the big surprise of the night was waiting outside. The limo was nothing impressive. Tuxedo black-and-white, short enough to be mistaken for a hearse, but providing the advantage of looking larger in the context of a bowling alley

parking lot. It would fit all of them, and it was a limo. The gesture was kind, so Jacqui, Amy, and Tammy all did their best, without conferring, to feign excitement and surprise in equal volume. This, of course, after standing around awkwardly while Kenneth passed the van keys off to his mother, who had shown up in her nightgown with a flannel over her shoulders, to collect them.

In the limo, Tammy declared, "I hope they play REO Speedwagon."

Amy rolled her eyes. "No way."

"Way. It's romantic."

"Excuse me?"

"It's romantic."

"REO Speedwagon?"

"Yeah. What?"

"Jacqui, back me up on this," Amy pleaded.

Kenneth, Marcus, and Bud were staring out their windows, pretending not to listen to the debate.

"They're fine," Jacqui answered, not wanting to take sides.

"Anyway, there's just one song I want to hear tonight," and it was much more romantic than anything REO Speedwagon had or would ever release. Their music was the kind jocks got laid to, and it would never be romantic.

"What song?"

Jacqui was deciding whether or not to share the answer when the limo shrugged into an abrupt halt, causing her to spill from the flask she was sipping from between conversational cues. Before she could say anything, the driver was pulling open the back door and yelling at everyone, "Get out! Now!"

Upon exiting the vehicle, initially unsure if they were being robbed or kidnapped, the group froze and observed the flames shooting from the cracks between the hood and the body of the limo. While everyone else continued to stare, Jacqui's eyes wandered to the limo driver with the car phone in his hand, the cord stretched to its full extent. She assumed a manager or dispatcher or something on the other end of the line, maybe the fire department. She turned and walked to the gas station across the street. At the pay phone, she called a cab.

"Actually," she added, turning around to see the limo now fully enveloped in flames and everyone else, including the driver, watching it with their arms akimbo, "can I make it two cabs?"

The boys weren't allowed a vote in Jacqui's decision to split the group, the girls in one cab, the boys in the other.

In their cab, Amy asked the other two, "So?"

"I feel like," Tammy started, looking at Jacqui to verify, "Kenneth isn't getting any tonight."

"He wasn't to begin with," Jacqui answered, adding another bottle of SoCo to the flask, her corsage and the dark obscuring her action from their cabdriver.

The girls had taken the first of the two cabs and made it to the dance before the boys. Tammy wanted to wait for them out front, but Jacqui said, "They'll find us," without meaning it or caring, and headed toward the entrance of the dance. Amy followed.

Upon entering, Jacqui scanned the crowd, observed the ocean of carnation-pink—held her judgment till later when she was alone in her bed—and spotted Howard and his date. Just as her song started to play.

She knew it from the first beats of the drum. She put a hand firmly against Amy's arm to suggest she not follow, and strode across the room toward Howard, who was making small talk with his date. Just before the first lyrics of the song, Jacqui had her hand on Howard's, her eyes on Suzie's glance of reproach.

"Would you mind if I stole a quick dance?"

Suzie's barely hidden scowl, her too-heavily caked makeup, the volume of hairspray in her hair all suggested that yes, she would mind. But Suzie managed a, "No," and a disingenuous follow-up smile. Howard noticed none of this. His eyes were on Jacqui's, half-confused, half-interested, escorted onto the dance floor as Madonna sang, "I see you through the smoky air, can't you feel the weight of my stare?"

The two had just started to sway together—one set of hands clasped, the other two on shoulder and hip, respectively, pelvises much closer than polite for two people who had shared barely a "Hello" before this moment—when Madonna explained, "What I'm dying to say . . ."

Jacqui and Howard maintained eye contact for the duration of "Crazy For You."

Kenneth and the other two showed up halfway though the song. While Kenneth stood and watched, Marcus and Bud stole off with Tammy and Amy.

When the song ended, Howard started to say something,

probably adolescent and unimportant, but Jacqui stopped him. She brought her face close to his ear, kissed its lobe, and whispered, "It's fine." Then she walked away, with all the satisfaction she had imagined and more.

That was her last interaction with Howard, who would marry Suzie, as Marcus would marry Tammy, and Bud would marry Amy. Jacqui was not often a topic in Howard and Suzie's home, but was a reason to spend an evening in silence each of the four times her name was mentioned during the twelve years of their marriage. Even into their twenties and thirties, Howard and Suzie's two daughters would occasionally wonder out loud to each other, "Who was this Jacqui person? What could she possibly have done?"

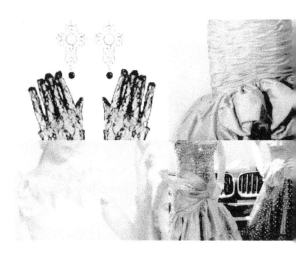

Before Madonna and Jacqui and Howard were finished dancing, Kenneth had excused himself from the dance entirely. That was the last Jacqui ever heard from him as well, excluding details through the gossip train of friends.

In the hospital bed in 1992, when Jacqui remembered her image in the Fletcher Bowl bathroom mirror, the thought inevitably leading to the rest of the night, a too-small part of her wanted to feel bad for Kenneth. But she didn't. She knew he was fine. He lived. Everyone lives, despite their fleeting, superficial pains.

And, most important to her, Jacqui would also live.

AVOIDANCE

Avoidance

KARA arrived at her slow-maturing appreciation for Maine only after graduating from Bowdoin. Between lectures, coursework, and the modest estimation of a social life, Kara managed to save enough money from her job at Hannaford to rent a summer cottage alongside a century-old mansion in West Bath.

Directly after the commencement ceremony, Kara's mother had asked her to move home, back west. She missed her daughter's presence, and the handful of times Kara was home—whether over summer break, or for Thanksgiving once and Christmas once—were not enough to compensate for her absence.

"Your visits are always so short, it just makes it harder for me," she'd tell Kara. She also believed, savings or no, that Kara couldn't afford the extra summer away. Her mother was right, but nevermind all that. Kara enjoyed a private stretch of beach, her own bathroom, and a kitchenette. And silence. She was able to spend three months on a schedule she dictated, seen only when she wanted to be seen. Hearing nobody, remaining unheard.

The most socializing she did was through letters she exchanged with friends back home, three sets of pen pal correspondences that she maintained all summer. It was an outdated format but she'd known the girls since middle school and they'd all held onto their passion for handwritten notes. One of them still indulged in surprise confetti. Kara found confetti surprises incredibly irritating, though less irritating than the harrying guilt of spending her last east coast summer apart from the peers with whom she'd shared the last four years. Flesh and blood friends, living in the same time-zone where she still resided. Kara kept telling herself it could wait, that she'd make time for them before the summer was over.

Up until the day she was in her car, driving home.

Sitting on a beach towel, writing her notes, Kara drank too much beer and gave herself heartburn, filled out in her hips and stomach, provided texture to the backside of her thighs. She spent humid afternoons watching the sky's movements above the bay, swatting at mosquitos and other winged nuisances. Some afternoons, she'd attempt to sketch the water in front of her feet or the sky overhead, but she wasn't skilled with drawing and always threw away her efforts.

Kara would remain on the beach until there was just enough light for safe passage along the trail back to the cottage, where she would read and accumulate empties until nearly sunrise.

•••••

Kara had worked part-time in her hometown before leaving for school. She appreciated the relative peacefulness her position offered, the brief interactions with patrons that didn't require genuine investment.

At Bowdoin, Kara had majored in Gender & Women's Studies and minored in Philosophy. That autumn back from school, she reapplied to her old job. On her first day back, a coworker—someone new, whom she'd never met, a young woman whose very buoyancy made Kara feel suddenly old, even at twenty-two—asked, "What were you planning to do with that degree anyway?"

Kara stared in silence as the coworker waited for an answer, realized one wasn't coming, and left the break room. She considered spitting in the coworker's coffee mug but decided against it and swallowed the mouthful of saliva instead.

When Kara's diploma arrived in the mail, she did not show it to her parents, didn't mention it. She put the stiff piece of cardstock back in its envelope and slipped it between some of her things in one of the boxes she was yet to unpack. There were five total, labeled with her name and what they contained. They were stacked in her bedroom, their sides slouching, corners crumpled in defeat. She hadn't really moved back into her old room as much as she was gradually unearthing her possessions and only as a need for them arose.

Each item she withdrew imbued the reality of moving home with greater permanence, a sense of backward momentum. Maine was in her past—four years that were now just a memory—and the likelihood of returning was less a reality with each day further from graduation.

•••••

Kara's acceptance to Bowdoin was well-deserved and she was successful as an undergrad. Still, she didn't make the experience as valuable as it could have been. There was no extracurricular activity, no joining of clubs.

In the four years she spent on the opposite side of the country, she rarely went outside to enjoy the differences. The snow and the cascade of autumnal leaves that preceded it were viewed from inside her room. If the syllabi allowed absences, she used all of them. Kara was lucky to have a dorm room to herself, where she could alternate between reading and staring at the wall without anyone around to ask what was on her mind. A scene from outside would sometimes catch her eye and Kara would observe life as it occurred for others.

The boys who found Kara attractive were the wrong ones. Some of them made her feel worse about her appearance despite being drawn to her. Whether because of the way they approached her, the topics they took interest in, their own physical features. Everything about them made her more aware of the scar framing her mouth. Any genuine effort put into a conversation would leave her feeling good about herself intellectually, but those thoughts were fleeting and, ultimately, more depressing still.

Kara attempted, a few times, dating women instead. They didn't try as hard and were a lot less stressful to be around. But after the third individual she realized that it was less about physical sex or gender and more a problem of vulnerability as a general rule, with any human. Kara did not enjoy the company of people, at least not as intimates.

The principle exception to Kara's solitude was the pleasure she took from the quad. There was a quiet to the quad that made it endurable. On her journey to or from class, she would go out of her way to travel through the expanse of walkway-gridded grass and trees, surrounded by old buildings dedicated to people whose names she did not recognize and whose accomplishments she did not care about.

On her adventures through the quad, Kara would deliberately favor the route that allowed her to pass the sign for Studzinski Recital Hall. It forced a smile from her, calling to mind an imagined Mainer equivalent of Jeff Spicoli—similar hair and demeanor, but a different accent entirely, and a Carhartt or L.L.Bean jacket in place of a Baja hoodie.

She was often, nearly always, en route to Benchwarmers, which had become her go-to spot, even if she felt out of place there. Kara preferred out of place over running into anyone she knew, suddenly forced to entertain the possibility of small talk.

She would sit at the end of the bar and pretend her best polite expression without inviting conversation, humoring a vague interest in whatever sports were broadcast on the television sets—always the Red Sox, always the Patriots—as cover for eavesdropping and people watching. And maybe the people at the bar knew who she was by now. They ought to have. But she wasn't obligated to them, as she wasn't obligated to her friends, the same who'd initially never wanted to join Kara at Benchwarmers, despite her reminders that "it's closest to campus." They always suggested some place further up the road, some place "more exciting." Whatever that meant and whoever cared.

If they spoke on the phone the next morning, if Kara mentioned stopping into Benchwarmers, her mother would always ask, "How was your lobster roll?"

"Mom. Why do you always assume I got a lobster roll?"

"Why wouldn't you? I would have."

"I know you would," which was only another among the things Kara had pretended she knew at the time. And anyway, Kara had burned herself out trying nearly every lobster roll in town by the end of her first semester.

•••••

Tonight, returning home from her shift, Kara longed for a walk through the quad. She would sometimes go out of her way north to Central Park, where she lingered around the monstrous statue of John Greenleaf Whittier—a poet admired by the Quakers, a man who never set foot in the town they named for him.

Or, depending on her mood and level of energy, she might cross Painter to wander aimlessly around Whittier College. But it would never be Bowdoin, nor would the night air feel the same on her cheeks or in her mouth, whether summer or winter. There were always too many cars on Painter, and it reminded her of traveling too far north on Maine Street, the busy part of Brunswick that her friends enjoyed, the stretch she chose to avoid.

Anyway, Nixon had attended Whittier College, which was enough to make her feel gross even being there.

"Better than Reagan," she said to herself, moving through dusk.

•••••

It was closing in on two years since graduation. Two years of texts that had gradually faded, of failing to save money to fly back for a visit. It wasn't going to happen. Not during the life she was currently living.

Kara would wait for her parents to go to sleep, before digging around inside the boxes. This was her routine. Her cat, Sylvia, lingered around the carpet of Kara's bedroom, slinking between the stacks she made in an attempt to finally unpack completely. Kara would look at her diploma, thumb through the books she'd kept, reread letters she'd failed to send, even with their envelopes already stamped & addressed.

She was back to living streets away from these friends now, and still neglected to spend time with them. The same way she'd avoided spending time with the friends who'd lived just down the hall in the dorms.

The dimness would creep and Kara would carefully place each item back in its box, as the absence of light penetrated her room.

Finally in bed, feigning sleep with Sylvia alongside her in the sheets, she'd replay in her thoughts each of her walks through the quad and plan her return to them. "Soon," she would tell herself, straddling the threshold of a dream.

MEANING AS USE

MEANING AS USE

KARA was shelving when Anne appeared at the end of the aisle and asked, "You speak sign language, right?"

Anne was not new to the library, but was hired before Kara returned from college.

"Anne," Kara had been told, "is your supervisor." Kara had nodded, discarded the information, and continued with what she'd been doing.

"Passably." Kara acquired her first book on sign language in middle school and a section of one of her bookshelves was now devoted to ASL texts, mostly unread. For a sixteenth birthday gift, her mother paid for sign-language classes at the Pasadena Language Center. While attending Bowdoin, Kara made the thirty-minute commute on Monday evenings to the Portland Adult Education Center, where she continued her study of ASL. But Kara was not deaf, and the rarely occurring exchange with a deaf patron offered Kara her few opportunities for unsure practice.

When Kara rounded the corner of the front desk, the librarians looked like they were shooing an animal out of the building. Kara wondered why nobody had asked him to write what he needed. She approached the man and waited for him to notice her standing to his left. When he sensed her beside him, he turned to face Kara and she signed *Can I help you?*

The librarians dispersed.

After she helped him find what he was looking for, Kara led the man to the checkout counter where she scanned his books and signed, *Due on the twenty-eighth.*

Thank you, he said and paused. She returned his pause.

He conceded, *Your name?*

K-A-R-A.

Thank you, K-A-R-A. He gestured at himself before spelling, *M-I-C-H-A-E-L.* Kara stared and he paused again before turning to leave.

Anne was already at the other side of the library so Kara went back to her aisle and continued shelving.

During lunch, Kara asked Anne, "Has the deaf man been in here before?" Kara reached into the bag of potato chips in front of her.

"I've never seen him before today."

Kara looked from the chip bag to Anne, who took a bite from her sandwich and chewed it. This was the only sound in the break room.

· · · · ·

That October, firefighters were failing to extinguish the expanding blazes north or south of Whittier. The evening news offered digital maps with poorly animated graphics to indicate threatened regions, borders of danger expanding from one broadcast to the next. The residue of summer that typically lingered into autumn was hidden from view before it was ready to leave. A potpourri of ashes and fallen leaves accumulated in the gutters, bristling whenever a car or breeze passed. The more acres the fire consumed, the more souvenirs the wind carried.

This—set to the backdrop of the widespread grocery strikes and the distinct possibility that Arnold Schwarzenegger would be the state's next governor—made Kara's return from school in Maine all the more surreal.

• • • • •

Kara set her things on the sofa and stepped through the patio door to the backyard. She did not brush the layer of ash—drifting from the sky, slim and cautious—from the lawn chair before sitting and lighting a cigarette.

Sylvia was in the grass, sluggish but feisty. A beetle landed in the lawn a few feet from the cat and his eyes shadowed the insect as it stumbled up grass blades that bent with its weight before giving way and dropping it from view. Its wings whirring from beneath its emerald and amethyst shell, the beetle lifted off for a moment before landing not far from where it began.

Sylvia crept closer. The beetle did not notice its peril.

The afternoon slipped into night. Kara showered and left her hair damp before climbing into bed. Sylvia crawled from alongside Kara's feet until his head was peeking out from the sheets beside her.

When he was through with Kara petting him, Sylvia burrowed back under the covers and Kara turned off the light.

There were no sounds from inside the house, but she could hear cars moving north and south along the cross street. Kara stared into the dark above her bed.

· · · · ·

Kara was seven-years-old when her parents took her and her older
brother to Big Bear. Her parents skied and Jacob chaperoned Kara on
the snow-tubing hill.

The hill was divided into four paths, each gradually steeper than
the next. The fourth path was marked, OFF LIMITS!! by a
hand-written sign staked into the ground. Jacob was bored after three
runs down the tamest of the slopes and had spotted the cautionary
sign from their first ascent.

"Are you having fun, Kara?"

She guessed she was, despite her cold cheeks. It took a moment to
choose her answer, and she nodded, unsure of what she was agreeing
to. She couldn't feel her fingers inside her mittens.

"Do you want to do something really fun?"

Kara wasn't sure there was any reason to say no and she trusted
Jacob, so she moved her chin up and down again.

"Grab your tube. Follow me!" Jacob made it sound like wherever
they were going would be one of the most exciting things they would
ever experience.

Jacob neglected to help Kara with her tube. It took Kara some effort to hoist it alongside her as she shuffled across the snow, the tube
bouncing off the side of her leg with each step. When they arrived
at the peak of the fourth path, Kara failed to notice the sign that had
drawn Jacob's attention.

Because of Kara's size, she needed help getting started, her butt
sinking into the open mouth of the inflatable inner tube, her feet jut-
ting into the air. Just before Jacob gave her tube a shove, Kara wished
she'd asked him to pull down the front of her beanie. It had ridden
up on her forehead and she couldn't do it herself with her mittens on.
She was worried she would never see it again, but didn't know she'd
never remember the beanie after this moment.

The reason for the sign was several sheets of fiberglass stacked at the base of the slope, unmarked and hidden by snow.

When Kara's tube struck the fiberglass, the top sheet snapped up and out of the snow. The cracked edge of the fiberglass caught Kara's upper lip and, as her momentum carried her seven feet into the air, tore to the base of her nostril where the edge caught and pulled the side of her nose apart. Kara landed separate from her left boot, blood spattered across the snow. Because veins and arteries had both been torn, some of the blood was dark on the white of the snow and other spots were brighter. Vibrant, oxygenated blood. Subtleties noticed by no one but the snow it melted into. Instead of waiting for Jacob, Kara stood and ran.

The further into the crowd Kara's uneven steps took her, the more people were pressing in around her. Some were yelling and Kara didn't know what she was doing wrong, why these strangers were upset with her. The escalation of confusion and noise was abrupt and Kara could only focus on running. No matter how fast she moved, there was red in the snow everywhere she looked. The crowd eventually closed in and lifted her into the air.

The sky above was gray and dirty compared to the white of the ground. There were too many faces looking at her and too many hands touching her. Her mouth and nose were hot and wet and stung when the cold air pressed upon them.

There were paramedics on the mountain and it wasn't long before a helicopter arrived to transport Kara to the nearest trauma center. Kara remembered little other than wanting to know where her parents were, wondering why her brother had abandoned her.

• • • • •

Dawn did not crack or burst like a hatching egg or crowning cocoon. It crept into the room in a procession of quiet gestures. Kara was soon more awake than asleep, her eyes discerning the shifts in light from between the blinds.

After fifteen minutes of looking at the ceiling, Kara slid out of bed and padded to the bathroom where she watched herself brush her teeth. She let her mouth hang slack, saliva and toothpaste rolling off the sides of her tongue into the sink. She splashed water around her lips and face before drying off. Kara manipulated her expression only enough to facilitate the application of makeup, careful not to disturb the path of her scar.

She preferred spending the most time on her eyes, which she believed distracted from her mouth. Depending on her mood or if she was running late for work—which was usually the case—this could involve any combination of mascara, eyeshadow, or eyeliner. The majority of the makeup ritual was foundation, to bring harmony to the blemished skin of her forehead, cheeks, nose, and chin, to camouflage her scar. This part was the same every day but the eyes could range from lazy to oddly ornate. No matter the degree of difficulty, there was always a messiness to it, which consistently included a change in skin tone where the foundation ended in an abrupt border just below her jawline.

At the library, Kara idled in a hushed walkway to read from a discovered selection. When Lauren approached to ask, "Remember the deaf guy?" Kara's shoulders tensed. "He's at the checkout desk." Lauren stepped out of view at the mouth of the aisle and Kara did not hear her finish, "I won't tell Anne you were reading again."

Kara placed her book on the cart instead of where it belonged on the shelf. After she made her way to Michael, she asked, *Can I help you find other books?*

Do you have a lunch break?

I have plans.

Would you like to get lunch with me tomorrow?

Kara paused, wanted to decline the invitation. *Okay. Can you meet at one?*

Of course.

I will meet you outside.

See you then.

Kara watched him leave. Once he was gone, she walked to the restroom. She stared at herself in the mirror for three minutes before rinsing her hands and placing them under the air-dryer.

• • • • •

They sat on the patio of Mimo's.

My hearing, my phantom limb. I walk down the street and sometimes I hear somebody call my name. I turn around, excited to hear a voice. Nobody there. I imagined it.

Funny, Kara signed. Michael looked at the ground, took a bite of his sandwich.

It had taken him a moment to decide how to sign *phantom limb* in a way that would express the intended meaning. When Kara misread his sign as ghost hand, Michael wrote PHANTOM LIMB on a napkin. She whispered it aloud, staring hard at the napkin. She set it on the table, closer to his side, and didn't look at it again.

He explained that he wasn't born deaf, but enough years had passed between hearing and now that his fingers had become his native tongue.

I keep the voices of my parents and sister in my head. When I imagine hearing a voice, I imagine one of theirs. If born deaf, I maybe avoid that feeling. I know people born deaf who dream in sign.

Kara missed details, didn't understand what he meant about dreaming, but pieced together what she could manage.

Do you read lips?

Harder than people think. Especially in a group.

Between the heads and the roofs of buildings beyond them, the smoke was layered thick enough to reach the gray of dusk, even at midday. Scraps of newspaper, fast-food bags, and unfinished cigarettes were buried in the ash that huddled near the bases of the shrubs and trees planted along the sidewalks of Uptown.

Before they stood to walk back to the library, Michael asked, *Do you have a partner?*

He'd immediately recognized the division in their fluency. It hadn't taken long for Michael to catch Kara missing her feeling fingers on words when the middle digits ought to have turned in, toward her chest. But she was here, having lunch with him.

Kara looked behind Michael, at a homeless woman across the street. The woman was holding a chocolate ice cream cone, gesturing at people with it. Everyone refused to acknowledge her or the ice cream melting down her wrist.

Kara looked directly into Michael's eyes and said, *No. I do not.*

• • • • •

"Well?" There were a handful of inquiries from her coworkers, all of them adding up to this single question.

"What?" Kara heard the flatness of her voice and immediately missed the thirty-eight minutes without it.

• • • • •

The fires were dying off. October passed and the winds with it, allowing the firefighters momentary advantages. The ashes were no longer being replaced after drifting away with the breeze. Blues and pinks returned to the sky's mornings and evenings, and the smoke washed out to sea and was erased.

The due date had come and gone for the books Michael checked out the afternoon he and Kara met.

The day before Halloween, Michael and Kara were on her living room sofa.

We should have planned earlier.

We could dress as—Kara stopped short, realizing how much spelling her suggestion would involve. She stood from the sofa and ran to her room, returning with a book each by Simone de Beauvoir and Jean-Paul Sartre. She pointed to their names and couldn't resist an eager grin at her own suggestion.

Michael's face already suggested he was unfamiliar with the names before he signed, *Who?*

Kara frowned and pulled a thread from a sofa cushion, unhappy further still because she didn't know the sign for the answer. She grabbed an envelope from the side table and wrote, *philosophers* on the back side of it.

Michael showed Kara how to sign what she'd intended to say, but she was feeling restless and didn't really pay attention.

They couldn't agree on anything and settled on improvisation. Kara found a pair of white bunny ears for herself and used eyeliner pencil to draw a villainous mustache on Michael. They finished him off with her beret.

Every year the owners of the home at the corner built a haunted house in their front yard. The trick-or-treaters and their parents were backed up in a small line branching out from the entrance. A steady current of artificial fog crept just above the wet grass. The candy-wrapper strewn yard was crowded with children, yelling in anticipation as they waited to get in. There were also exhausted cries from those who'd already endured the maze.

When it was their turn, Kara and Michael made their way through the makeshift scare house. Kara held Michael's hand and counted the times a sudden sound caused her to start while he remained unfazed.

After they exited, Kara asked, *Can we get food?*

At Al's they split an order of onion rings and a grilled cheese. In the red baskets they left behind on the aluminum-edged Formica table, Kara's napkin was mangled, crumbs clinging to its edges. Michael's was folded in half, marked by eight greasy fingerprints and the wide smear of his mouth. Neither signed during the meal.

•••••

November.

Kara couldn't reach a conclusion about Michael's interest in her. Each time she considered asking him, she decided there was no point. He could like her if he wanted. She had enough trouble deciding how she felt about him.

Apart from his hands, Kara's sense of Michael remained vague. She knew his face, but there was little distinct about him beyond his deafness. To her, he looked like any other man in his early thirties. He was not unattractive, but nobody would point Michael out to a friend or imagine him while they masturbated. Kara and Michael had fucked by now and it wasn't bad. But Kara believed that if Michael could hear, they might never have spoken and never screwed.

The more time she spent in Michael's company, the less Kara spoke and the more she muted her already dry voice in the rest of her conversations. There were times when she could tell her co-workers thought she was trying to prove something through her dispassionate silence. She was, but she didn't prefer to think of it that way.

•••••

Her shift ended and, as Kara approached the exit, she thought about Michael's inability to hear her. His understanding of Kara would remain different from everyone else's. She didn't want to be only the sum of her appearance and the inexperienced motions of her fingers.

He was waiting in the parking lot, staring at the roof of the library. Kara turned to see what he was looking at, but saw nothing.

When they got to his apartment, as if making an important announcement, she signed, *Tell me what you hear when you imagine my voice.*

What do you mean? I do not hear.

Kara thought back to their lunch date, when Michael said he sometimes heard voices in his head. He may have used the sign for *hear,* or maybe she had just read into what he had shown her. She tried to recall how Michael's hands had looked that afternoon, but could produce only an anemone of fingers.

What about the voices on the street? Have you thought of my voice? Her questions crowded as she rushed through clumsy signs.

Michael's expression hadn't shifted and Kara let her hands fall silent. Instead of signing what she thought she felt, she just said, "Sorry," to herself. One short sound in a too quiet room.

Michael appeared to be at once pitying and unsympathetic. *Why do you think I imagine your voice?*

I did not think about my question.

Michael frowned, weighing his thoughts before he signed, *You should go.*

Why?

You make a point to convince everyone of your depth. Too naïve to understand you seem arrogant.

She was already opening the front door when he snapped his fingers. The sound was abrupt, obstinately loud. Kara turned to face Michael.

He kept his eyes on hers. *Even with your unpleasantness, I stay around because I feel warmth. But nobody likes waiting. Only you care about the sound of your voice.*

Kara's hands wanted to lift from her sides, but Michael stopped them by signing again. *I stay open with you but you keep distance between us. You know about my scar, what about yours?*

Kara just stood there. Everything she was feeling, she didn't have the confidence to sign. There was too much of it. She started, *I.* What could she say? She pushed the front door closed. *Can I use your bathroom?*

His expression said he didn't want her to, but he signed, *Okay.*

At 6:33 P.M., Kara screamed louder than she ever had in her life, then sat on the bathroom floor and wept. Michael's neighbor, Gerti, heard the scream, chose to ignore it, and never mentioned it to Michael.

Ten minutes later, after rinsing her face, Kara returned to the living room and sat on the floor directly in front of Michael. She let their eyes match for a few seconds before signing.

I went sledding as a kid. I crashed into a pile of wood that tore my face open. It took a long time to look like this.

Now Michael didn't know what to say. His anger had already settled while he was waiting for her to exit the bathroom. Kara continued, *I have a bad habit of starting projects and giving up. I have many things unfinished.* Kara stretched her fingers in front of her and drew in a breath. *My aunt hosts Thanksgiving. I want you there. I want to make a dish with you. I never wanted that.*

He didn't pause before responding, *Of course.*

Thank you. He looked like he was waiting for her to say more. She noted the time. *It would feel good to stay, but I'm tired and need sleep.*

Michael nodded and stood. *I understand.* He kissed Kara on the cheek, then on the lips. *We both need rest.*

He opened the door for her and Kara stood in the doorway to look at Michael before signing, *Goodnight,* stepping outside, and letting him close the door behind her.

The street would have been completely silent, were it not for the light rain falling or the streetlights whirring behind it. As she started her walk home through the mist, Kara smiled and the skin pulling taut around her scar felt unfamiliar.

JOHN CHRISTOPHER NELSON'S youth was split between ninety-four acres of chaparral in East County San Diego and a defunct mining town in the Nevada high desert. He has moved thirty times and currently lives in West Seattle. He earned his BA in American Literature from UCLA and is a graduate of the Stonecoast MFA in Creative Writing. His work has appeared in The New Guard, Able Muse, Chiron Review, The Matador Review, Indicia, Parhelion Literary Magazine, Necessary Fiction, Broke-Ass Stuart, and elsewhere.

NANCY PEACOCK

ALICIA HOKANSON

Gathering
Reunion
Blueprint

GATHERING

1.
At Equinox, the slant of light changes
but keeps its strict appointment: seven to seven.
Brilliant days still hooked to summer
come edged in cold and shadows
that cover half the beach.

Fall raises the curtain
on the losses to come, as crackled leaves
curling along the grapevine
crumble into the flax and lithodora.
The cats bat them across the withered lawn
where walking brings gold spiders down.

And summer's toll keeps piling in my heart:
my first lover dead from ALS, a dearest friend
gutted by pain, gone by her own hand,
my love three weeks adrift in hospital beds,
our nation's fabric fraying at the edges —

And now the doctors in their crisp shirts
have said the radiation didn't work, the tumor
grows and soon our beloved uncle will need
all our care to help him to the door.

2.

Carrying her dead calf
the mother orca follows the pod
lifting the body
up to trailing whale boats,
tourists, helicopters —
          to our sight-seeing push,
          our engine clatter,
          our pollutants filling the waters —

She bears her calf for 16 days,
for a thousand miles,
up into the human world
crying
this, this —
She is our activist
in grief and rage
carrying a dying planet
on her rostrum —

3.

September coals fall to ash
in the creaking stove, and the days
are measured out in chores:

I've gathered five bins of apples to the press,
two dozen jars of cider canned,
and still one tree's so laden
I can't pick them all myself.

I've gathered, too, some sunsets
burning a fierce horizon,

gathered in a full moon washing
squares of light across the floor,

gathered morning fog in the clearing
to store this forest silence
for our darkening time.

REUNION
Manzanita, Oregon

Ocean waves wash in without ceasing,
curl and break — sunlit blue
or greyed-out in the rain,
they collapse on themselves,
and dissolve in thin foam on the beach.

It's easy to let them be background noise,
enjoy the wide view without really feeling
their unrelenting pulse pummel the shore.

In the good-bye bear hug
from your dearest nephew
suddenly the tears press out.

Why is it only in the kindness of others
that this grief rises to the surface?

A glance, a hand squeeze,
that more-than-expected embrace
from your young oncologist
catches me out and I am pulled
into the undertow.

In the sweetness of this gathering:
your children and grandchildren
your siblings, your nephews,
the whole rootball
of ex-wives, half-brothers, near sisters —
it seems no one but me
shies away from a straight-on look
at your coming death,
though all week the sea
has chanted it in my ear.

BLUEPRINT

I've found that favorite photograph of you—
your face shadowed against the plywood
of a wall you've just raised:

bare-chested, hammer in hand,
jeans powdered with fresh sawdust,
you lean against the studs,
your bitterness dissolving in good
work, in building something wholly new.

This refuge carved out of time,
out of fir and moss
in the clearing of an abandoned orchard:
agate light, eagle feather,
sea breeze from the north—
our house in sunlit woods.

Those years of building were your therapy.
Jumble of tools after each day's work,
my clean-up job. Under this roof
we hold each other's histories.

Now you tremble on your cane
and the long bandage of your grief
unwinds itself from the bone.

SHERRY RIND

Poems based on antique science
Scitalis
Elephants, Their Capacity
The Reverend Alexander Ross Explains Griffins
Saint Ambrose Admonishes
Castor

Scitalis

> *The snake called scitalis gets its name because it glitters*
> *with such a variety of colour.* Aberdeen Bestiary, 1200 CE

He cannot join your drinking parties
your warm rooms lit by fire.

Beneath notice
he puts all effort into his dress

gold and diamonds, a glimpse of peacock blue
leaving you hunting for the rest of the bird

or maybe a butterfly, you think.
Blinded by sunset pink and copper

you slow. He's just here, down here
among the multitudes

the mud and moss where desire starts.
It tricks you awake, holds you

mesmerized. And then
he has you.

Elephants, Their Capacity

The elephant is the largest of them all, and in intelligence
approaches the nearest to man. Pliny the Elder

You will never speak our language
which is of the earth
the deepest tides of underground streams
the molten shiftings you cannot hear.
We speak to the lines of sound
among planets, thin as spiders' silk
when the new moon reveals itself
after the darkest night.
Silver to silver
we send up the water
and return to the forest.
Thus, we mark the years
of ascending and descending on earth.
When one of us falls,
we inhale her scent to keep it
with the other stories.
We know every story is much the same;
the follower is not less than the leader.
When you take one of us
she will learn your language and obey
because she is no longer herself
but a dog whose world is work.
Because you fear our size
you diminish us.
Because you cannot hear
you do not know how the earth talks to itself.

The Reverend Alexander Ross Explains Griffins

*Besides, though some fabulous narrations may be added to the
story of the Griffins, as of the one-ey'd Arimaspi with whom they
fight, yet it follows not that therefore there are no Griffins.*
Alexander Ross, Arcana Microcosmi, 1652

At the edge of the inhabited world
where all things most rare and beautiful are found,
near the cave of the north wind, Boreas,
that violent old man of wings and ice-spiked hair
whose sighs hurl men off mountains,
where griffins build their lairs high above his cave,
the Arimaspi men whose desire has no end
crawl up in search of gold.

A thousand men wait for a moonless night
to invade with spades and sacks
but if one should ring the silence with iron on stone
the sharp-eared griffins rise on thundering wings.
Plucked up like mice, men break
with cries that rumble down the mountainsides.

Made wealthier by danger, those who escape with gold
say the griffin is lion bodied with an eagle's head,
claws the size of drinking cups,
black feathers along its back,
white wings, and eyes like fire. Do they fly
or leap with claws outstretched
so far that those who fall in terror
believe them airborne? Do their eyes burn red
or reflect mere firelight?

Though fearsome beasts grow larger in the mind,
it does not follow that they cannot be.
If any say such animals as griffins
are not found in our civilized world, I say it may be true
for they live in places so remote —
and many there still are —
that Europeans dare not pursue a welcome
and only the gold descends into our hands.

Saint Ambrose Admonishes

Whereas [crows] offer even their own lives for strangers, we close
our doors to them....Whereas the storks consider these as
their defenders, we frequently treat them as enemies.
Ambrose of Milan, 4th century CE (approx. 387)

When the year begins to close,
storks in migration do not rise
like wind-tossed leaves

but, following the guidance of crows,
advance in precise ranks
of military pageant, their wings its banners,

their guardians ready to battle any birds that close
against them and to see their charges safe to winter roosts.
The crows do not linger in pleasant climes

but, covered with the wounds
of bitter conflict, return to the cold, crying out
encouragement and pain to one another.

Is there punishment for desertion from this dangerous bond?
To keep from harm, do some crows hide as the rest fly off?
No, each strives to outdo the others in his allotted task.

Whereas crows offer their own
lives for those not of their flock, we bar our doors
and hide as if in fear. We shirk the duty owed

the stranger and the oppressed (except the odious
Jews whom we consign to the flames
for their refusal to be saved in the sight of Our Lord).

Although animals lack the wit to question their lot,
we with superior powers are raised above all others
to reject their ways or honor them as beacons

rising in a world granted as our dominion.
Following, we claim the wealth
found even in the wings of birds.

65

Castor

He throws away that, which by natural instinct he knows to be
the object sought for…. Gerald of Wales, 12th century CE
The Itinerary of Archibishop Baldwin through Wales

The one who draws the short straw
must lie on his back and accept
all the timber piled on his belly,
arms and legs held up like the sides of a cart
and his mouth stuffed with sticks
before his compatriots drag him by the tail
to their river den where several families
together make their dwellings
wherein they sleep upstairs when the water rises
and below when water recedes.

Like the frog or seal, these animals
remain under water at their pleasure,
guided by broad, thick tails.
Because this part is naked, great
and religious persons in time of fasting,
eat the tails as having both the taste and color of fish.

The beaver digs dry hiding places in the river bank
and when he hears the hunter
seeking him with sharp poles thrust down the dirt,
he flies to the defense of the castle;
but if he cannot elude the hunter and his dogs,
he will ransom himself. In the hunter's sight
he castrates himself with his teeth
and throws the testicles to the man
who will sell them for medicine.
If the hunter pursues a castrated beaver,
the animal at an elevated spot lifts his leg
to show the object of desire is gone.

The beaver has but four teeth, two above and two below,
broad and sharp to cut like an axe.
When a beaver can get hold of a man,
he will not let go
until he hears the fractured bones
grating beneath his teeth.

These five poems are part of a manuscript based on natural history from ancient Greece and Rome to the Middle Ages. In some cases, the intent is to show how some attitudes persist. In others, such as "Saint Ambrose Admonishes," I turn the writer's words back on himself.

SHERRY RIND is the author of five collections of poetry and editor of two books about Airedale terriers. She has received awards from the National Endowment for the Arts, Anhinga Press, Artist Trust, Seattle Arts Commission, and King County Arts Commission.

BETWEEN STATES OF MATTER
A Poetry Box SELECT title | Published Spring 2020
https://thepoetrybox.com/bookstore/between-states

points out that we spend more time getting somewhere than being there, more time in the process than the final form. And beings are always trying to upend the way things are, whether it's a lion appearing in the front yard, a plant sneaking out of its assigned place, or the author shifting between her own self and a dog.

CARBON RINGS

SCOTT EZELL

—Isaac Asimov, *Short
History of Chemistry*
We're journeying constantly, but there is
always a machine and books, and your body is
always close to me...
— Henry Miller, in a letter to Anaïs Nin
...is the carbon molecule lined with thought?
—Saul Bellow, Herzog

CARBON RINGS
Allotrope: [from Greek allotropos 'of another form,' allo-
'other' + tropos 'manner,' from trepein 'to turn']
Each of two or more physical forms in which an
element can exist. Graphite, charcoal, and
diamond are allotropes of carbon.

IRON
IN PURE FORM
IS NOT VERY HARD.
However, an iron im-
plement or weapon may
pick up enough carbon
from charcoal to form
a surface layer of the
iron-carbon alloy
we call STEEL.

CARBON RINGS

THIS IS ONE OF SIX CYCLES OF POETRY
CALLED CARBON RINGS BY SCOTT EZELL.
THIS CYCLE IS COMPOSED OF FORTEEN POEMS.

1

Carbon bonds with itself and other
elements, creating ten million known
compounds, more than all other elements
combined. Carbon rings are the basis of
life on earth.
I once worked in a machine shop
subcontracting for the military — I
breathed burnt metal
as it rose off steel lathes
and painted oil on diamond bits cutting
threads
in F-16 engine rings.
Sawdust spilled across the floor, clotted
with oil and zinc spurs. I soaked
sandpaper in kerosene to polish grooves
in slabs of armor plating,
day by day
the skin peeled from my hands.
After the shift bell
I drove home on six-lane freeways,
streams of head- and tail-lights slipping
through the dusk, undulating over desert
hills, backdropped by the sea.
Hubcaps spun like centrifuges on the
wheels of trucks, carbon precipitated
on the lips
of exhaust pipe bores.

2

Carbon compounds include hydrocarbons,
the chief components of fossil fuels, and
esters, which give flavor to many fruits.
Crankcase oil fills my mind, spills down
my neck and spine and flows
to the swell
of your belly and breasts,
the hollow where the tendons of your
thighs converge,
the two-tongued flower
opening the seam
of you
to me.
You are a flesh kiva, jar of salt and blood
buried in the earth — I come to you
from the stain of metal days
and descend
through hair and skin
through the press of flesh and fluid to
where our bodies merge into
a rush of color
a flush of light
a bath of ash and grease.

3

Some carbon compounds are lethally
poisonous (cyanide) and some are essential to life (glucose).
The city is a grid
of fog and emission haze, boulevards of
lights and engines run and tumble to the
sea.
Beneath a freeway overpass
a Christmas tree
lies discarded on a curb,
still nailed to its wooden cross.
A motel sign blinks
NICE, CLEAN
in flashing neon,
as a man shuffles through a dog park
pushing a shopping cart
piled high with blankets and cans, ice
cream cone melting in his hand.
The LA River curves through canted
and beveled
concrete banks,
tanker cars rattle over
rust and weeds,
an alluvial fan of tracks.
Next to a freeway on-ramp
a palmtree stands
on a burned-out slope,
a million cars drive by,
automatic sprinklers chuck and turn
speckling the ash.

4

Carbon-nitrogen compounds are
extremely unstable, so can be used to
make explosives, such as TNT and
nitroglycerine.
Banality of armageddon, metal bubbles
roll down asphalt streets, the drone of
a power mower fades across a quilt of
lawns, lips suck
gasoline and wine
through plastic tubes
as bombs explode next door ten
thousand miles away, waiter another
round
this is an excellent vintage, newsprint
confetti
a parade of meat,
avenues littered with desire.

5

Carbon was not created with the origin
of the universe, but is produced at the
core of stars.
I love to push the breath out of your
body,
then feel it lift and fill against my chest.
The extremity of me emerges radiant
from you, seeds of our union
spill across your skin,
I put my mouth
to your ribs and thighs and swallow
the space between us.

6

Some plant biomass is eaten by animals;
some is exhaled as carbon dioxide; some is
dissolved in oceans; dead plant or animal
mass may become sedimentary rock or
fossil fuel.
Sub-Urban Vehicles are army trucks
painted lipstick colors,
machine sex
of pistons and bone,
an iron Buddha sits beneath a gum tree in
a square of grass,
crows swirl above an intersection,
alight on power lines that
pulse with uranium heat—
elsewhere,
stealth bombers glide
on steel wings above Sumeria,
cuneiform wedges pressed in clay, exhale
carbon gas into the stratosphere,
open bomb bay doors onto Mesopotamia
horses pull carts piled high
with cotton bolls,
men play songs on instruments
of hide and bone,
and girls dip buckets
into stone-lined wells,
scour cooking pans with sand,
talk and laugh as they
delouse each other's hair.

7

In the crust of earth, carbon compounds
occur in minerals such as marble, magne-
site, limestone, chalk, and in fossil fuels.
Outside the Hollywood Greyhound station
sidewalks are embossed with
round black stains
of chewing gum
and bronze stars for tv personalities.
Skinny knees beneath a miniskirt, a girl
jangles
like a pocketful of change strutting past
window displays of leather, feathers, and
high heels, a kid in a flannel shirt
sits against a parking meter playing Jimi
Hendrix
on a cheap guitar,
Foxy Lady you got to be all mine,
HUNGRY
on a piece of cardboard propped against
his boot,
cowboy hat
upturned to the sky
in a prayer for
money or rain,
OK! tattooed on his wrist in ballpoint ink,
either he's from Oklahoma or everything's
alright
or both,
I drop him some coins
and step inside to buy
a ticket to San Francisco.
On the Greyhound,
it's a methadone migration ($C_{21}H_{27}NO$)
in cheap shades and denim jackets, as if
we're movie stars
slumming on the bus for kicks,
stare out the window
stoned with bovine mass transportation
blues, I-5 north out of town

men and women in flotsam shelters
trees with yellow leaves
on silt islands
in the concrete bed
of the LA River.
Up the long low grade of the Grapevine
pass, striations of rock twist open into val-
leys, game trails crisscross ochre soil and
high-tension power lines swoop through
on totemic towers of steel geometry.
We crest the pass
with a caravan of flatbed trucks
hauling concrete culvert pipes, lime green
grasses grow
around the burnt stumps of a wildfire,
descend
through a veil of mist
to the Central Valley,
vineyards pin-stripe the distance as far as
I can see.
Pit stop, Cohuenga Junction,
stand in the parking lot
puffing cigarettes, back in the bus
nicotine breath fogs the windows,
fast food burger smells spread down the
aisle.
A tractor combine ruts
the valley up into rows for crops,
we drone past acres of orange trees staked
out in a grid that shutters through, leaves
snapped brown by frost.
Clouds of dust
blow across the interstate, 10,000 cattle
low
in a feed lot of mud and shit, tendons
straining in their necks, veins of snow

gleam
where the Sierra
lift their bulk of rock and light
above the valley haze.
The hammer arm of an oil pump
rocks up and down
sucking crude from the crust of earth,
a satellite coasts across the purpling dusk,
a flock of starlings
swirls like a river
churning and twisting above an aqueduct,
halogen lights illuminate the belts of a
gravel factory, windmills line a crest of
hills.
We turn off I-5 and follow another set of
power lines west to San Francisco, edge of
the continent,
end of the trail,
the start of new migrations,
topsoil washing to the sea,
sex and machines and alcohol and time
climbing up the shore in waves.

8

Under terrestrial conditions, conversion
of one isotope to another is rare, so for
practical purposes the amount of carbon
on earth is constant.
Girls in leather and high heels model
porcelain smiles
for a photoshoot,
still life with
cigarette butts and dried gum, a
helicopter,
noise insect of metal flight, rises from a
freeway bridge into a slab of yellow
evening carved from the underbelly
of the fog.
Skyscrapers yawn and stretch,
pull on plaid slacks and golf cleats and
stride
into the sea
with a jangle of spare change and keys,
discount coupons in their wallets,
black Xs in all the square days of the
calendar.
Tanker ships anchor high and empty in
the bay, floating ghost towns off the
waterfront. Construction cranes
sweep the sky
above a parking garage,
a dozen levels of chrome and engines me-
tered with hours
between white lines.
Newspaper headline 25 cents, turn the
page you see
burned bodies decompose
in desert light,
shells of shiny char.
In a back alley
an old Chinese dishwasher smokes next to
a dumpster,
black letters on a cinderblock wall say
NO STOPPING ANY TIME.

9

Produced by living things, carbon dioxide
is a minor component of the atmosphere;
plants draw CO_2 from the environment
and convert it to biomass through
photosynthesis.
I didn't build
the pipelines of crude
that bisect and tangle continents,
or cast the veils of radiation
that cling to soil and leaves and skin.
I wouldn't strike a match
to set the earth on fire,
but with every breath
the world burns for my subsistence.
Sometimes I feel like a wounded king
descending into earth —
iron arrows converge upon my chest,
gasoline fumes undulate
from my lips and tongue.
Forests fall branch by branch from my
heart, mountains stand up and walk away.
Pipelines bisect my body,
veils of radiation sheathe my skin.
Who conceived
the square-cut towers we live in? I don't
desire them,
but they are built by my desire.

10

Most carbon-based compounds do not
break down in water. Water does not
dissolve our skin because skin is made of
carbon compounds.
Napalm,
toss a dash
over your shoulder
to make up some luck for what we've
spilled—
benzene polystyrene gasoline,
shake it up and pour,
a cocktail of carbon rings
that sticks to skin and burns.

11

The paths that carbon follows are called
the carbon cycle.
My bones and engines sink in mud
for future time to burn.
I will be a tongue of gasoline, a tongue of
fire
to lick, taste, embrace you,
I will break
the glass of desire like a window
open
for us to step through to the sky.

12

A hydroxyl is an oxygen atom bonded to a
hydrogen atom—when joined to carbon in
a molecule it makes alcohol.
"Fuck the government" says a man
smoking in the doorway of a bar.
The Transamerica Tower broods in a sea
of fog,
spare changers in baseball caps shake
nickels in soft drink cups, drink malt
liquor
by a chainlink fence.
Men push crates into metal sidewalk
chutes, spitting in gutters and speaking
Cantonese,
a girl with pink hair
and a heart tattoo
wanders a heroin dream, picks through
shards of glass for the shine of coins.
Jackhammers rip up asphalt, backhoes
reach
beneath the city's skin
to scoop out piles of earth.
"It's pouring," someone says. Outside the
sky
falls
over
San Francisco.
In the doorway of the bar
the man lights another cigarette, says
"Fuck the cocksuckers,"
and the jukebox sings,
"looks like nothing's going to change,"
so I remain,
order another round,
outside the window
cars and buses
drive on through the rain.

CARBON RINGS

13

CARBON IS
ABUNDANT
IN THE SUN,
STARS, COMETS,
AND IN THE
ATMOSPHERES
OF MOST
PLANETS.
TEN BILLION
YEARS
THIS CHAOS
SPUN IN
CIRCLES
TO PRODUCE US

at the seam of
sea and sky, your
breath rising
and falling like
rain across my
chest, sun and
almond blossoms
washing over us
in waves.

14

Allotropes of Carbon:
Diamond is the hardest known
mineral, graphite is among the
softest. Graphite is an excellent
lubricant, but diamond is the
ultimate abrasive. Graphite
conducts electricity, diamond is
an electrical insulator. Diamond is
transparent, graphite is opaque.
We come from chemical bonds,
independent pieces linked
into a ring, stacked
and braided into patterns—
tapestries of fur, marl,
cirrus clouds, diamonds painted on
a water jug, a coil of clay
smoothed into a hollow, skin
stretched over ribs.
We began from sludge and muck,
climbed fish ladders of
intestines and erections
through hair and teeth in piles of
scat—20,000 years ago
we crossed the Bering land bridge
dressed in skins and grasses
to emerge
with lips of chrome and rust,
burning mesozoic heat.
Sometimes I feel alone
at the edge of this continent
where my leaves all fall and rustle
to the sea,
but how could I be far from you?
We are allotropes of one another,
pterodactyls rise from exhaust
pipes to the city sky,
I saw a thousand birds
fly through a thousand windows
but really it was you.

the ITALIAN QUARANTINE

by
BARET MAGARIAN

Previously published in **WORLD LITERATURE TODAY**
with photos by Pierpaolo Florio | March 23, 2020

A novelist living in quarantine in Florence looks back at Italy's cultural history and then forward, considering whether something positive might rise from the ruins that the virus will leave in its wake.

*L*AST WEEK I VENTURED OUT OF MY FLAT IN FLORENCE, ARMED WITH MY AUTO-CERTIFICAZIONE, THE DOCUMENT you must possess in order to justify leaving your residence at any time in locked down Italy. As I cycled, trying to snatch a few minutes of permitted daily exercise, I veered for the Piazza del Duomo. I glanced around nervously, on the lookout for any abnormalities, policemen, anxious to avoid any official entanglements or questions. My exodus was marked by the electric flutter of adrenaline. As I gingerly reached the geometrically intricate miracle of Brunelleschi's dome, I realized that I shared the square only with a military vehicle and some soldiers; no other civilian could be seen. It was disquieting. Did I mention the silence? It was cosmically still, as if I had just alighted on an alien planet that housed a carbon copy of Florence, but utterly bereft of sound and people. Just now the real Florentine sun is starting to ripen and ferment, settling into its springtime incarnation, and as it touched the upper levels of the Santa Maria del Fiore Cathedral and the gargantuan dome that sits atop it, a dazzling, magical clarity resulted. But there was no one to share the moment with. I was alone.

SOLITUDE. This is the inalienable fact of the Italian lockdown. We are all alone suddenly. Ordinary men and women alone in their homes, critically ill patients alone in hospitals (for those who are battling the Covid-19 virus are strictly isolated because of the risk of infection; not even relatives or parents are allowed to remain with them), and those shoppers who must remain at a meter's distance from one another when they go out for essentials like food and medicine. The only places that remain open in Italy are pharmacies, supermarkets, bakeries, tobacconists, and newspaper kiosks. One of the cruelest privations in terms of everyday social interaction for the Italians—and for me, for that matter—is the loss of the ritual of the espresso, taken at the bar. The very few souls one sees outside are more often than not masked, wary, jittery. I was chastised by one man for walking too close to someone else the other day on a street that was otherwise deserted, like every other street in Florence. At a bakery, a member of staff insisted that I step back from the counter. When I did as she asked she insisted I step back further. To have stepped back any further would have required the demolition of the wall.

FOR ITALIANS, WHO ARE SO GREGARIOUS, SO PHYSICALLY demonstrative, so loquacious, able to throw a party anywhere, even on a street corner, it is a cruel, surreal plight that they suddenly find themselves in. And the city's ethereal beauty now feels almost sterile without the complementary babble of human emotions and voices that it ordinarily generates. Florence has become like a colossal movie set, after having been abandoned when the production money didn't come through, an open-air theater for no one. While it is true that its almost metaphysical beauty and purity can now perhaps be apprehended the more clearly, the absence of humanity is elegiac. Perhaps we realize that beauty is inevitably diminished when it is glimpsed in isolation from others.

FLORENCE HAS BECOME LIKE A COLOSSAL MOVIE SET, after having been abandoned when the production money didn't come through, an open-air theater for no one. It is difficult now to imagine that only two weeks ago the city was so different, filled with tourists, all galleries and cinemas and bars and restaurants open, sounds of traffic, street life, singing filling the air. But it's not just Florence, it's the whole of Italy. At first it was only the northern region of Lombardy that was placed under quarantine, and in Tuscany we felt some pangs of guilt about that region's restricted life. Then on March 9 the prime minster,

Giuseppe Conte, ordered that the whole of Italy be placed under a lockdown after thousands of Italians fled from the north to Puglia and Calabria. They wanted to reunite with their families, stirred to panic-filled action after there was a leak about the projected quarantine in Lombardy from the League, the opposition party. Conte's decision was the only real option available to him, for people had now grasped that the most serious thing about the coronavirus is its terrifying level of contagiousness. The next day, Conte ordered the lockdown to go into a higher gear—restaurants and bars that were allowed to stay open until 6pm the previous day were now ordered to shutter completely. Tourists were ordered to leave, hotels and Airbnb's emptied instantly.

BY THEN THE ITALIAN GOVERNMENT HAD ALREADY been accused of having messed up, shutting the door after the horse had bolted. It is true that a national alarm had been sounded in January when the virus was first detected to have traveled from

Wuhan to Italy. Perhaps a quarantine could have been instigated earlier. In his defense, Conte has displayed exemplary transparency in terms of the communication of his intentions, not electing to disappear whenever the going got too tough. He has proved to be more of an old-fashioned statesman than his counterparts in Europe and America: the UK, for example, is a hothouse of rumors and ambiguity, as Downing Street invites selective journalists to relay its incoherent messages. Similarly, the Italian medical sector—one of the finest in the world, and free to all—has been admirably professional and composed, despite the staggeringly difficult circumstances in which it is now having to function. Bergamo's deaths are happening now so quickly that the cemeteries and crematoria simply can't keep up, and the military has been called in to intervene and help.

THE POST OFFICE ALWAYS USED TO BE A BIT OF A GOSSIP center where people stopped and chatted, and business was conducted at a leisurely pace. On the whole, by all accounts, the Italians' sense of civic duty has been good. Italians were never a populace fueled by a strong sense of social awareness; they were noted for their defiance, their contempt for authority and rules, but now they seem to be united by a common respect for one another and a gentle persistence and determination to do the right thing, to be considerate of others. I went to my local post office a few days ago, which is still functional but now ruled by a new protocol: one must wait outside in an orderly fashion, observing the one-meter social-distancing rule, and then only go inside when another customer comes out. The post office always used to be a bit of a gossip center where people stopped and chatted, and business was conducted at a leisurely pace: now everything has become Calvinistic and severe. But it's an admirable method; to be overtly emotional now would be disastrous.

SIMILARLY, THE STAFF AT SUPERMARKETS, THE PHARMACISTS, the medical personnel that I have spoken to: they all give off an air of stoicism and resilience. When I took the time to sincerely thank one of the exhausted supermarket staff for his unfailing efforts to meet the needs of his customers, he just brushed off my gratitude modestly. And no one has been panic-buying, at least not in Florence: once Italians were reassured that the supply of food would be constant, they could relax. I spoke to a freelancer in film production based in Rome, and he told me that the Romans have been obeying the rules and keeping their distance. He didn't think that there was a risk of eventual anarchy breaking out, since Italians are serene by nature, unlike the more volatile Anglo-Saxons. Others I spoke to, such as a language teacher and translator, based in Lucca, found herself missing terribly the screams of her students, camaraderie with colleagues, and the colorful mess of school life.

AN INTERESTING QUASI-PARADOX ABOUT PRE-LOCKDOWN Italy is that while bureaucracy was always labyrinthine, glacial, and elaborate—when paying in cash to an Italian bank account, for example, you had to produce your medical card with your tax code and your identity card—everyday life was structured around the concept of improvisation and the idea of making it up as you go along. Now, in lockdown, Italy improvisation's spark has been snuffed out. But a sense of social responsibility has hesitantly slipped into the space improvisation once occupied.

BARET MAGARIAN is the author of *Mirror and Silhouette*, a novella set in Venice; the novel *The Fabrications*; and, most recently, the story collection *Melting Point*.

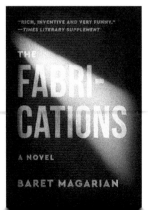

"RICH, INVENTIVE AND VERY FUNNY."
—TIMES LITERARY SUPPLEMENT

THE FABRI-CATIONS

A NOVEL

BARET MAGARIAN

IT'S SCARIER BECAUSE IT'S SO TIMELY.
HOW WOULD PEOPLE REACT IF THE
CORONAVIRUS GOT WORSE...
RATHER THAN BETTER?

SUGAR MOUNTAIN
by ALFRED ALCORN

AUTHOR SYNOPSIS:

Set in the near future, *Sugar Mountain* is a saga about the struggles of an extended family to survive a lethal avian flu pandemic. Within days, the world changes radically and forever as the infrastructure of civilized life crumbles. In short order, there exists no power grid, no internet, no media, no medical facilities, dwindling supplies of food, and, for most people, very little hope.

A committed pacifist, Cyrus Arkwright has been preparing for several years to make Sugar Mountain, his ancestral farm located in western Massachusetts, into a self-sustaining haven for his extended family. He is, in the modern parlance, a "prepper," one of the growing number of Americans (that range from the militant right to the communal left) who are getting ready for some kind of apocalypse.

As the family in-gathers during that calami-

I read *Sugar Mountain* on my Kindle and couldn't put it down. It was utterly gripping and frightening (thanks a lot!)... But oh what a grim subject, which I take to be on the edge of allegory. Thank you for sending me the book. —*Lloyd Schwartz* / I just finished it...a riveting read...better than many "best sellers." —*Bob Viarengo* / I am addicted and cannot put it down. —*Philip Lovejoy* / I stayed up until 2:00 am to finish the book last night, I couldn't put it down. I loved every "page." It was fantastic. And I loved Allegra's journal....Great book. I want to see the movie. —*Anna Doyle* / Just wanted to say that I read four chapters last night and am thoroughly hooked. The characters and their plight stayed with me today. Can't wait to continue! —*Jennie Summerall* / But what a page-turner this is! Beautifully written literature....The suspense in unstoppable; the multitude of characters flawlessly orchestrated; there's a New England aura to it, and Allegra's diary is a wonderfully pinned-down example. I love every minute of it and I am only at page 216. —*Stratis Haviaris* / Unfortunately, this absolutely could happen either in the way you write about or as a natural mutation in the virus. —*Stephen J. Gluckman*, Professor of Medicine, Perelman Medical School at the University of Pennsylvania; Medical Director, Penn Global Medicine

tous May when a deadly form of H5N1 begins its destruction of the human world, the Arkwrights are not only besieged by pleas from friends and loved ones, but realize they are vulnerable to the violence and lawlessness that is spreading with a contagion of its own. Having laid in supplies, devised basic systems, and established a self-sustaining farm, Cyrus, his wife Grace, and their three sons and their families become prime targets in a ravening world.

As national, state, and local governments shrivel to all but non-existence, it falls to son Jack, an Army Ranger veteran, to organize the defense of Sugar Mountain. It is Jack, over the protests of his father, who earlier acquired a store of weapons and now teaches the others how to use them.

The principal threat to the refuge arises in the form of the McFerall brothers. Men in their late fifties, Duncan and Bruce live with their families in a hollow several miles from the Arkwright refuge. For more than a century there has been a festering feud between the two families as to the ownership of Sugar Mountain. Empowered by the possession of stolen antiviral medicines and as a member of the National Guard, Duncan is in a position to command weapons and men. In the guise of suppressing "terrorism," the brothers launch a systematic campaign of attacking and taking farmsteads in which they place their retainers. Sugar Mountain is high on this list.

In its situations, in its characters, *Sugar Mountain* explores the human species in extremis—that is, in those conditions that existed through most of our evolutionary history.

READER COMMENTS:

In its situations, in its characters, *Sugar Mountain* explores the human species in extremis— that is, in those conditions that existed through most of our evolutionary history.

DAVID GROSSKOPF

November 9th, 2019

RIPENING

Stephanie would walk with my humbled body,
pacing my uneven stride as my shoulders pitched up
to the beat of an impinged nerve throbbing
under the tight strap of a cloth brace,
and my right good arm hooked on her left
down the street lit by sunlight against a gray sky
that deepens hues and sharpens lines of every
leaf and steeped roof.

Shoulder to hip among neighbors and trees,
we'd walk and speak of leaves and of sunlight,
of sky and wood sashes, speak of nothing;
I'd reach for colors of a tree on fire and speak them.

We will lean like this when we are old, I thought,
and we will walk slowly and witness slowly
and we will own every color
and every brittle crust underfoot.

And what of the year now past?
It brings health.
It brings memories of a car and a crumpled bike on a blinking road.
It brings Stephanie, and daughters, and friends.
It brings these leaves
this year and every year and every year passing:
red more vibrant and leaves more red—
leaves variegated and proud.
Stephanie and I will walk through them and say,
Look at the color on these leaves!
—no need to say anything new.

JOHN DELANEY

WISHING STONE

A ring of white quartz

orbits this grainy stone

beached at my feet.

I place it in my palm,

so smooth and round,

exquisite and well-traveled,

squeezing till it's warm.

My wish is its mission now:

to see the world before I leave it.

I throw the stone back

to the armless ocean

and let the waves,

as they are destined to,

retrieve it.

ESTHER COHEN

posts a poem a day at
ESTHERCOHEN.COM
Every Single Day

1

WHY THERE'S A POEM TODAY

because this afternoon there will be rain

because I am meeting Marianna for coffee

because Ahava's taking dance class

because I can watch the movie DIANE

because maybe I'll make Julia Child's beef stew with small pearl onions

because our neighbors will come for a holiday drink

because Saturday is the day to rest from the news

because last night we celebrated birthdays with old friends

because I miss my friend Linda

because there is a new foot massage place on Broadway

because I saw Jerry Garcia once a long time ago

because there are four library books next to my bed

because we have smoked salmon for breakfast

because even on Saturday there are poems

LIKE AND LOVE

not a Noah Baumbach fan

Marriage Story last night

liked it enough my favorite actress

from Nurse Jackie played Scarlett J.'s sister

and I wondered about whether it is possible

to dissect Like and Love to really know why

Some People for instance the woman who came

to visit yesterday she came with friends to

an impromptu writing class in the living room

told her story about living in the car with her dog

for 18 months on 233 Street in the Bronx near the cemetery

some people you just Love Right Away not because

of their story although for sure that is a part of love

and then some people, Adam Driver with A Very Good Nose

some people you Like Well Enough

but it doesn't much matter if you see him ever again

3

DEAR PERSON WHO IS WONDERING
WHAT TO DO ON HOLIDAYS

IF YOU AREN'T RELIGIOUS

IF YOU ARE A LITTLE BIT RELIGIOUS

IF YOU DON'T HAVE A BIG FAMILY OR A SMALL FAMILY

OR A FAMILY AT ALL IF YOU DON'T KNOW A

LOT OF PEOPLE IF YOU ALWAYS THINK TO YOURSELF

WHAT SHOULD I DO THIS IS A HOLIDAY

MAYBE EVEN A BIG HOLIDAY NOT HALLOWEEN

OR TU B'SHVAT DEAR PERSON WHO WANTS

TO CELEBRATE BUT IN A MINOR WAY TO LIGHT

A CANDLE OR TWO OR THREE BECAUSE

IT'S ALWAYS A GOOD IDEA TO LIGHT A CANDLE

AND EAT A MEAL ANY MEAL

MEXICAN FOOD OR A BIG BOWL OF SOUP OR VEGETARIAN PAELLA

FOOD IS FESTIVE JUST BECAUSE IT'S FOOD

AND INVITE A FRIEND TO EAT WITH YOU OR MEET YOU

SOMEWHERE ANYWHERE I LIKE TO MEET

IN CHINESE RESTAURANTS ON HOLIDAYS

THE WAY MY ANCESTORS DID (!!) AND GO

TO MOVIES BECAUSE EVEN A BAD MOVIE

CAN BE A GOOD MOVIE AND BECAUSE A HOLIDAY

IS A CELEBRATION NOT JUST OF WHAT MIGHT

HAVE HAPPENED BUT OF WHAT CAN HAPPEN

TODAY AND TOMORROW AND THE DAY AFTER THAT

IF WE CELEBRATE WITH A CANDLE AND A MEAL.

4

IF I DON'T WRITE A POEM

it doesn't mean I don't want

to disorganized a person who

lives with no straight lines I do not

have routines or plans do not have

anything alphabetized in order in a row

Yiddish word is farmischt and yet

because there is always always an

and yet even on those days when I can not

for reasons of no reasons, write a poem

and yet there is always underneath the surface

where good words live there is somehow

always even when you can't see it

a poem.

5

A PARTY FOR JOE

Saturday Joe celebration
Joe loved parties people discussing
everything he danced
with Annie last New Year's Eve at a bar on 72nd Street
liked going to lunch to dinner even breakfast
see movies plays curious and full he always carried
a book with him Joe knew how to love and all the people
who came to have a drink or two or three to Joe
at the Water Club on the river a Joe day they all
loved Joe still do his party was perfect
beautiful skies open bar white roses piano player who knew
every single Cole Porter song Leonard Cohen too
in his tribute Joe's grandson Corey called Leonard Cohen's
songs geriatric erotica Joe would have loved that
end of the program Annie maybe she is
an angel on this earth Annie as beautiful as Annie
Joe loved Annie Annie loved Joe Annie read
Joe's last poem called Ummm because he couldn't remember
but he knew he loved poems, wanted to keep reading them
out loud to strangers wanted to live and live and live. He does.

6

ALL HOLIDAYS HAIKU

We should celebrate
lights and trees and you and me
whatever we can

7

A MOROCCAN MAN AND
WOMAN I DID NOT KNOW

met them at a party last night
he gave me his Arabic translation
of T.S. Eliot's Four Quartets his wife
a book of her Arabic poems I did not
bring my books for them
trays of food hard not to eat it all
deserts from phyllo dough honey and nuts
orange slices with cinnamon
stories of life and life here
for four years from Morocco for work
three boys rented house in Pelham
round and full entirely present arms open wide
my first trip to the Middle East crazy impossible
place hard not to want to live there
with people like this man and his wife and yet
she's been in New York four months now she said
Anyone Would Want To Live Right Here.

MICHAEL DYLAN WELCH

GRACEGUTS.COM

....

FOUL BALL

The sun cuts through the trees to the side of the left foul line. A twelve-year-old leans forward over home plate, cocked and ready. The pitch hurtles straight down the middle—whack. Curving foul, to the left. A toddler beyond the fence stays crouched on the grass. The pop-up arcs its way down. At the last minute a man lunges. He does not try to make the catch but thrusts himself over the boy. He takes the ball hard in his back, then his momentum carries him past the toddler and he falls with a howl onto the grass. The toddler looks up, a plucked dandelion in his pudgy hand.

FAMILY BUSINESS

My undertaker uncle hadn't seen a shooting victim for years. He said it would have to be a closed casket because the guy'd been shot in the face. Only twenty years old, in the 7-Eleven for a slurpy. Uncle Phil comes over for dinner once a month, when it's dad's turn to host poker night. Mom asks him not to tell these stories but we always ask. Every week, Mom feeds everyone her banana-nut bread, except for Uncle Phil, who's allergic. Last week Mom said that she wants to be cremated, but Dad says that wouldn't be good for his brother's business.

NAKED

It's a story about my childhood, and I tell it to you on our first date because you said you'd visited India last year. As a child, visiting Calcutta, I had seen a dead baby, face down and covered with flies in a cardboard box, the box wet from the muddy gutter it lay in. We share other memories, other details of ourselves. You tell me of the time you climbed your brother's favourite tree and found a magazine stuffed into a hole, a National Geographic with pictures of topless African women. Later that evening I wonder if I'd always imagined my story from a picture in a magazine, and what you meant by your story, what I meant by mine.

AWAY

eastward-bound—
a gibbous moon
reflecting on the wing

        lights of an unknown town
        through a break in the clouds

the sun's last rays
catching the fuselage
of a jet above us

distant thunderhead
glowing for a moment
with lightning

        rumours back home tonight
        of the aurora borealis

sudden turbulence . . .
in the dark
I whisper your name

While we never find out why Ponicsán feels bad about his dick, we do find out a lot about a writer who's been turning out award winning screenplays and fiction for years. This book, a light-hearted send up of Nora Ephron's, *I Feel Bad About My Neck* finds Ponicsán waxing alternately philosophical and vinegary as he takes us on a trip through Hollywood's movie business, the Watts riots, breakfast cereal, sex and invasive medical procedures. There are engaging digressions into the life of a script doctor, politics, porn, the benign-neglect style of parenting his folks practiced and the beauty of non-attachment. He moves it all along smoothly, never letting truth stand in the way of a good story. If you've ever wondered what Jack Nicholson's like, or who buys lunch when the players in the movie business go out to eat, or what the screenwriter of The Wild One said just before he died, this book is for you. You couldn't call it memoir but then again, why not? Whatever you call it, at fewer than a hundred and fifty pages, it left me wanting more. If you like charming stories, good writing and a few laughs, ignore the title and buy this book.

-BRADY T. BRADY, has published short stories in the anthology Editor's Choice III Fiction from U.S. Small Press and in the Hawaii Review and the San Francisco Reader, among others.

DANCER IN THE GARDEN
JUNE 15, 2020 | DR. SIEGFRIED KRA

Author of *TWILIGHT IN DANZIG*, a captivating, cinematic novel leading up to his prominant, industrialist father and family narrowly escaping the gestapo at the beginning WWII and fleeing to America as a young boy. Based on actual events of his Kra's life.

"Just touch him," I tell the masked and gloved figures. "Hold his hand and it will give him a feeling of comfort and security. He won't be so frightened. It's an old method I learned in medical school, before you had all these machines." All medical care should include the ancient bedside practice of taking the patient's hand. "It works better than Xanax," I tell them.

From suviving a plane crash on a frozen lake to a sanatorium in the Alps, with the antiquated mysitque of sunlight and rest as the cure for TB—which is about all we can do now with Covid-19 until we get a vaccine and proper medicine—where he falls in love with a ballerina, too soon to die. One of many captivating, dreamy stories, gliding you into a past world of short stories from a Doctor's notebook.

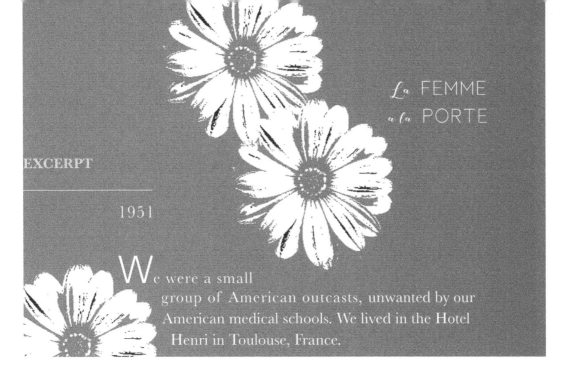

La FEMME a la PORTE

1951

We were a small group of American outcasts, unwanted by our American medical schools. We lived in the Hotel Henri in Toulouse, France.

I had graduated from CCNY and was labeled a radical and a Communist because I had participated in the riots in our school to oust an overtly anti-Semitic professor. The McCarthy years produced hosts of casualties, but for me they ushered in an exciting opportunity.

all the other students, I had a miniature kerosene burner on which to brew coffee, fry eggs, and cook hamburgers in a cast iron pan. Given the inexpensive French bread, cheeses, and wine, I made do on seventy dollars a month.

I covered the walls of this tiny room, and even the ceiling, with blackboards that I filled with formulas and detailed drawings of nerve connections for my anatomy class. I wanted to be surrounded by their names and images so they would become as much a part of me as my arms and legs. The first thing I saw when I awoke each morning was the arterial supply of the stomach, which spread across part of my ceiling. This room became my sanctuary—at once my library, dining room, sleeping quarters, and a place to dream of someday becoming a doctor.

Our hotel was small, located one block from the Place Capital, the center of the city, run with a warm hand by a gracious concierge and his wife. They lived in an apartment on the ground floor, immediately behind the circular desk of the lobby.

The least expensive rooms were small, but opened on an enclosed central court with a large circular skylight. I lived, uncomfortably, in one of these rooms. It had a sink, a bed, a large armoire with a full-size mirror, and a small desk. Like

FORTHCOMING AUGUST 15, 2020

For the common folk, life was filled with hardship and constant struggle: most importantly the struggle just to stay alive. Famine and poverty were rampant as well as lawlessness. One's life was always at risk from marauding bandits. The only safe havens were the abbey and, living under the of auspices of the clergy, one was subject to their avarice and their corruption, and their often ruthless and hypocritical behavior, as young Cuthwin learned as a young boy, when he ran away to escape being brutally flogged for imitating the untoward behavior of one of the abbey's guardians.

THE LIFE & TRAVELS OF SAINT CUTHWIN takes the reader through eighty-five years of Cuthwin's life, which was filled with both misery and happiness, great loss as well as great love. The reader empathizes with Cuthwin as he struggles to stay alive, scavenging for food like an animal and seeking shelter in various abbeys and camps. We experience his joy when he falls in love and marries, as well as his sorrow when experiences heart wrenching losses that were so common for the average man who fell victim to hoodlums, gratuitous killers, foreign enemies and the unscrupulous power-hungry abbots themselves. "Writers must believe what they write," says Warner; "otherwise, they don't write at top form. When something devastating happens to one of my main characters, it is almost akin to having it happen to a living person in my life," he adds.

THE LIFE & TRAVELS OF
SAINT CUTHWIN by Irving
Warner, who Library Jour-
nal hailed as a *"[combination] of
Hemmingway and John Steinbeck."*

This novel is a virtual time machine
that takes the reader back to 11th
century England—the time of Sax-
on domination before and after the
disastrous Battle of Hastings in
1066.

Step directly into the footsteps of
Cuthwin of Alnwick. There are
few "great men or women" in this
historical novel, but instead the
story of an ordinary man and his
wife who work to survive.

Cuthwin, who dictates his story
around his 85th year of life, scru-
pulously avoided people of great
power and standing. As he told his
wife, the fiery Cwenburh, "such
folk as we, are pebbles and dirt under heavy merciless wheels of great
men and women."

IRVING WARNER

The Life & Travels of
Saint Cuthwin

A medieval tale of love and conscience.

"If one were to combine the creative genes of Ernest
Hemingway and John Steinbeck, the result might just be
Irving Warner." –*Library Journal*

www.CUTHWINandCWENBURH.com

101

"I AM HOPING THAT WHEN THE CLOUDS AND THE FOG OF THIS PANDEMIC WAR DISSIPATE, THERE WILL BE TIME ENOUGH TO TAKE STOCK OF WHO WE ARE AND WHAT IS LEFT FOR US TO DO, GIVEN OUR GIFTS AND OUR VISION." -From Robert Karmon, author of *Isaac,* in an email.

ROBERT KARMON is an award winning playwright, published poet, short story writer and published screenwriter, who has worked on screenplays for Columbia pictures, CBS and Eddie Murphy Production.

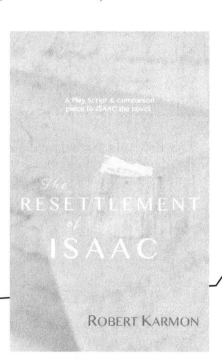

Including an additional five chapters before the war as a youth.

"I was immediately drawn into the plight of this brave young man as he learns how love and friendship can overcome the memories of hatred, discrimination, and terrible loss. is is a masterful coming-of-age novel amid the horrors and passions of war."

~ DICK ALLEN, author of *Present Vanishing, Ode to the Cold War, is Shadowy Place,* and Connecticut State Poet Laureate (2010-2015)

THE SEQUEL TO *ISSAC* / STAGE PLAY
"THE RESETTLEMENT OF ISAAC"
TO BE PUBLISHED THIS JUNE.

FROM ANNEMARIE HAGENEAARS WHO PLAYED TWO OF THE LEAD ROLES IN LAST SUMMER'S PRODUCTION.

"We will perform it at the third annual Jewish Film Festival in Southampton on August 21st, directed by Robert Kalfin (founder New York's Chelsea Theatre Center, winner of five Tony Awards, four Tony nominations and 21 Obie Awards).

I am truly astonished by Karmon's book [Isaac]. In Dutch we have an expression that says: "This book reads like a train". And it means that you can't put it down once you start reading. It is exactly what happened to me."

https://annemariehagenaars.nl/2017/08/02/double-role-in-stage-adaptation-of-novel-isaac-by-robert-karmon/

In concert with this year's film festival we are pleased to present the Playwright's Theater of East Hampton's premiere staged reading of "The Resettlement of Isaac". This play is based on the true, incredible story of Isaac Gochman, a 17-year old from Rovno, Poland, who, in one horrific night, survives a Nazi massacre of his entire family along with 20,000 other Jews.

Thrust alone into the forest and the wilderness of war, Isaac finds the courage to fight back as a Russian partisan blowing up Nazi trains, and finds the passion to fall deeply in love with Anya, a Russian partisan nurse — in love for the first time in his young life. It is a tragic love that transcends religious differences.

Many years later in New York, the elderly Isaac is still haunted by the memory of his first love. His only friend, a young German-American woman, is tormented herself by doubts about her father's role as a German soldier during the war. Deeply affected by Isaac's past, she becomes the loving caretaker of his memories after he is gone. The play confirms what Faulkner once wrote, "The past is never dead, it's not even past."

Concrete Art Space,
Alsekar Avenue Arts District
Sharjah, UAE
Nov 10th, 2019

LARA SWIMMER PHOTOGRAPHY
www.swimmerphoto.com

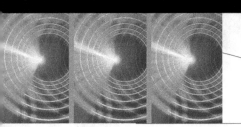

THOMAS WALTON is the author (with Elizabeth Cooperman) of *THE LAST MOSAIC* and *The World Is All That Does Befall Us* (Sagging Meniscus Press). He is one of three editors/contributors of *MAKE IT TRUE MEETS MEDUSARIO* (Pleasure Boat Studio, 2019), a bi-lingual poetry anthology, and author of the micro chapbook, *A NAME IS JUST A MANE* (Rinky Dink, 2016). His work has been published in numerous journals, including *ZYZZYVA, DELMAR, BOMBAY GIN,* and others. He is founding editor of *PAGEBOY MAGAZINE* and teaches math in Seattle.

WALTON'S SEVENTEENS
  WILL BE PUBLISHED THIS
  SUMMER AS A COLLECTION,
   ALL THE USELESS THINGS ARE MINE
  (SAGGING MENISCUS, 2020).

DRAWINGS *by*
JASON
BLOOM, a sign artist
for Trader Joes & other
establishments.

[seventeens are mini-poems composed of 17 words, like a modern-day haiku, but with less rules.]

When the sun broke like an egg over the field I JUST ATE AND ATE AND ATE.

{ WE BURIED THE RAINCLOUDS
UNDER THE DOGWOOD
WITH A SIGN THAT READ:
Here Lies Last Night's Storm. }

I wonder if you can still buy beachballs — do they exist? — now that I'm living in Wyoming.

WE BURIED THE RAINCLOUDS UNDER THE DOGWOOD WITH A SIGN THAT READ:

Here Lies Last Night's Storm.

Do you really think this is the only chance you have at life, just one, then, nothing?

I wonder if you can still buy beachballs, – do they exist? – now that I'm living in Wyoming.

When the sun broke like an egg over the field I JUST ATE AND ATE AND ATE.

I RAN OUT OF THE GARDEN SCREAMING, *the hydrangea's blooming! the hydrangea's blooming!* "the hydrangea's blooming!" PANTS AROUND MY KNEES.

The green water holds well a white sailboat proud as a clit in the thickly wooded cove.

BESIDE THE EASY FLOW OF THE SHALLOW CREEK THE EASY FLOW

of the 'round 'rocks waved hello.

The green water holds well a white sailboat proud as a clit in the thickly wooded cove.

I RAN
OUT OF THE
GARDEN
SCREAMING,

"THE HYDRANGEA'S
BLOOMING!
THE HYDRANGEA'S
BLOOMING!"

PANTS
AROUND
MY
KNEES.

Do you really think this
is the only chance you
have at life,
        just one,
                then,
    nothing?

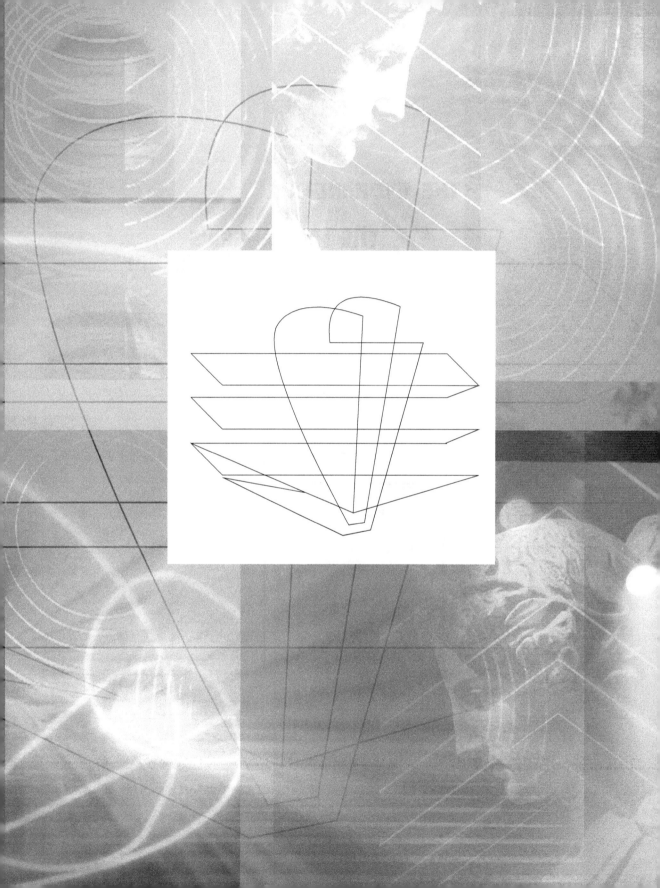

JARED LEISING

Containers
There's No Secrets in the Kitchen
The Rising Cost of Intuition
Wearing a BABYBJöRN®

CONTAINERS

"When the source being documented forms part of a larger whole, the larger whole can be thought of as a container that holds the source."
—MLA STYLE CENTER

We've always been the source
of something—
of your caliber, whose
internal diameter

self-regard, loathing, loanable
funds—but what
doesn't evade larger
questions like

larger whole can contain us?
What Netflix
I do. I'm sorry, maybe
I've got it

movie are you? The birdbox
"was invented by
all wrong, maybe we're
Russian dolls,

the British conservationist
Charles Waterton . . .
made by Russian trolls—
or just yellow

to encourage more birdlife
and wildfowl."
onions. That might
explain the tears.

More life, more fowl
play w/language

I shouldn't be using
around a person

THERE ARE NO SECRETS
IN THE KITCHEN

I don't like to sit

I like to think
of words
dying in the air

After work
I do landscaping

I walk in the forest
unfolding layers
of reality

a filigree of veins

and green
if you count
the leaves

I set my patience
in a spider's web

hoping it stays put
but it blows out
so I place it back

in my pocket

until the wind
dies down

THE RISING COST
OF INTUITION

You know

without knowing why
      you picked her
out of a line up to perform in
      the orchestra for the blind
you'll be conducting
      like the invisible gorilla

you understand

      you are becoming

the shooter—you can feel it
      in your gut,
texting while driving,
      exonerating the brain
from its primal, petty
      conversation

with the road and your eyes

      as you retake

the SAT in the middle of
      a rock concert
that is your smart, new life —
      a daily admission
exam in which you forget
      the playlist

and stick with your first answer

      far too often

instead of going back
      and making
the necessary corrections.

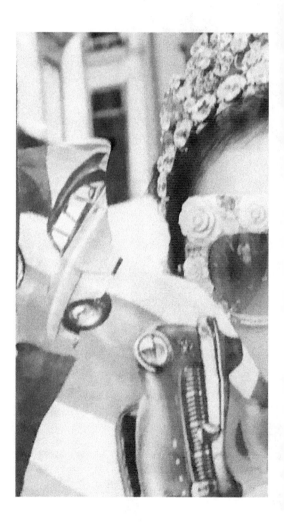

WEARING A BABYBJÖRN®

into a liquor store with your five-month-old
facing the thirsty horde of George C. Scotts
and Betty Fords, like a chubby, ruddy shield.

The undead stare, as they should: you are sad,
a young man with a soft sacrifice strapped to
his chest, and you are searching for anything

that's forty proof. Speaking of which—you've
forgotten your identification, which you realize
as you pull a bottle of bourbon off the top shelf

—but you have a baby for God's sake. Isn't that
proof enough of your manhood? You squeeze
the expensive vessel by its red, waxy neck

and approach a register, getting in line behind
Liz Taylor and Richard Burton who are reloading.
Your son makes prehistoric sounds at a window

and it's hard to say who is more of a man—you,
George C., or the woman who is carrying nothing,
pushing a stroller past the store without stopping.

Previously published by OOLIGAN PRESS in
Alive at the Center, an anthology of poets
from Seattle, Portland and Vancouver.
https://ooligan.pdx.edu/book/alive-at-the-center/

JARED LEISING grew up in the Midwest, and is the author of a chapbook—The Widows and Orphans of Winesburg, Ohio. Before moving to Seattle, he received his MFA in creative writing from the University of Houston. In 2000, Jared began teaching English at Cascadia College, and continues to do so. For the past few years he's also been coteaching a creative writing class for women at the King County Jail.

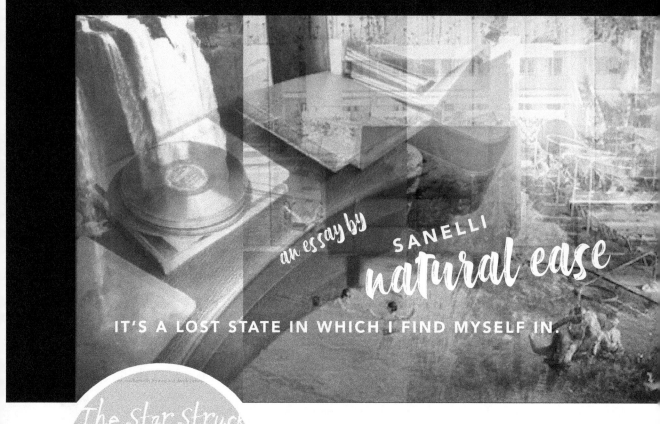

an essay by SANELLI

natural ease

IT'S A LOST STATE IN WHICH I FIND MYSELF IN.

The Star Struck Dance Studio

I don't really know how to be here, how to fill the hours. I am staring out the window a lot and thinking about who else is eyeing the same turbulent sky.

As fulfilling as my recent book launch was (except for the one Q & A at Elliott Bay Book Company where I knew before even calling on the man-whose-hand-shot-up that he would tell me what he didn't like about my book and why), it still stands out as one of the most uneasy times in my life. I had worked so hard to prepare which excerpts to share. But all through the weeks, on some innate level, the realization that once it was over the whole cycle would need to begin again: writing something to be proud of, selling myself as not only a decent writer but one with a successful platform, the logistics of putting together another book tour, well, I slowly began to appreciate how much work it is to live up to the demands of the process.

My friend Steph said I look relaxed, but the outside of someone is often so different from their inside.

None of us should let fear lift us from our roots, from what grounds us and lets us flourish. But when your work is what makes you feel most alive, to find yourself suddenly out of its tumult can create a windstorm of its own.

I think most writers can relate. I take great comfort in this.

To ease myself, I've decided to meet my friend Bob for coffee, something I seldom do. He loves to meet for coffee, but it isn't like this for me. I think about it, but the part of me who prefers spending mornings at home in her sweats generally wins out.

But Bob is someone I can unwind with, settle down into myself and be real. So with two creamy caffeinated equivalents of dessert, we head down to the Water Taxi that will whisk us over to Alki Beach.

I believe that there are everyday events that we sense are enlightening even if we don't yet know what they are about to teach us. Just that they will.

This is what happens when I spot the little girl wearing a Shayla—hair, neck, and shoulders covered—sitting crossed-legged with her family (men, women, numerous children) on a huge woven mat under a wide blue tarp secured by the weight of halved Clorox bottles filled with sand. Between them, a feast is spread in large tinfoil containers. The food smells so good, Bob and I spend a long moment inhaling its tang. "Do you think they could be our new best friends?" Bob says.

I shake my head because it occurs to me that there are scores of twenty/thirty-somethings moving to Seattle from all over the world to work at Amazon, yet I rarely see an entire family together.

When I say as much to Bob, he changes the subject. Not dismissively, it's just that one mention of the word "Amazon" can send him into a tailspin. "Doesn't it strike you as funny to see Bezos's empire rise from the depths of Sixth Avenue after he convinced all the independents that no one needs a brick and mortar presence anymore? And now they are the biggest brick and mortar presence this city has ever seen?"

Bob's insights are some of my favorite understandings of how the world works. Like my trusty flat iron, I rely on them to set things straight. To tease, I say, "Modern times paging Bob."

"Sorry," he said, and then quickly returned to what I'd said about families. "Whole families arrive here together, but they tend to live south. An economic wall divides Seattle, north from south. Take the light rail to the airport if you don't believe me."

"It's always been this way," I say. "The high cost of living defining what neighborhood we live in."

"I think it's more about ethnicity."

He's right. Growing up in New York taught me the importance of the word. How people want to live around their own no matter how often we throw the word integration around.

Even so, I find the division unsettling. Seattle is supposed to be better than this. We can't keep dividing up the world. It's all one big mess.

Under the tarp, the men throw arms around each other easily and often. Everyone is singing. I think, what language are they speaking? Have they found their way here from Africa by way of Europe? I'm staring now. When one of the men smiles at me, I quickly turn my head away.

I look around. Most people sit separately staring at their phones. No one is singing, not much laughter. The volley ball game is intense.

Watching the girl and her mother eat something I don't recognize, expertly with their hands, brings a shudder of nostalgia to the surface.

The reason? My own mother had a stroke of which she never recovered. She lived for another year, yet she did not. It's amazing how quickly we can lose ourselves.

I try my hardest not to let sadness sweep in, but it's too late. I'm too near the edge. Ut oh, I think, here it comes.

And it's not much help that I am suddenly thinking about one particularly sensitive nurse who squeezed my shoulders and coaxed me gently away from my mother's bedside, saying, "how nice a walk outside would be."

That squeeze kept me sane.

We gather up our things and Bob and I walk toward the Water Taxi, but before we turn to go, I see that the girl's dark purple head scarf has fallen to her shoulders but no one in her family seems to mind. I am really glad to see her whole face.

I knew I'd been waiting for something or someone to show me how pointless it is to worry, I just needed to get out of my office, stop thinking.

I think best when I'm not thinking.

Turns out it was this girl. When she shakes her hair free, the natural ease of that simple gesture touched me just enough to keep my fears at bay.

What I wanted from the day was respite.

What I got was so much more.

MARY LOU SANELLI has published seven collections of poetry, three works of non-fiction including AMONG FRIENDS (a Goodreads notable title), and her first novel, THE STAR STRUCK DANCE STUDIO of Yucca Springs, was recently released by Chatwin Books. She has contributed to the Seattle Times, Seattle Metropolitan magazine, Morning Edition: National Public Radio, KUOW FM, Crosscut, and has presented her work at Town Hall Seattle. Her regular columns appear in Pacific Public newspapers: The Queen Anne/ Magnolia News & City Living; in Art Access, and Dance Teacher magazine. For more information about her and her work, visit marylousanelli.com.

Of THE STAR STRUCK DANCE STUDIO OF YUCCA SPRINGS: Mary Lou Sanelli brings a depth of light and warmth to her writing. It's as if all her dancing has kept her afloat no matter how hard a circumstance. Maybe it's her Italian heritage too, (read AN IMMIGRANTS TABLE—wonderful poems of an old Italian and new Italian world with memories and recipes). This book's centerpiece focuses on healing through close ties, dance and self-acceptance from personal issues to brutal hate crimes...and how sometimes certain people deserved to be kicked out of a place, and sometimes others deserve forgiveness even if some actions are unforgiveable.

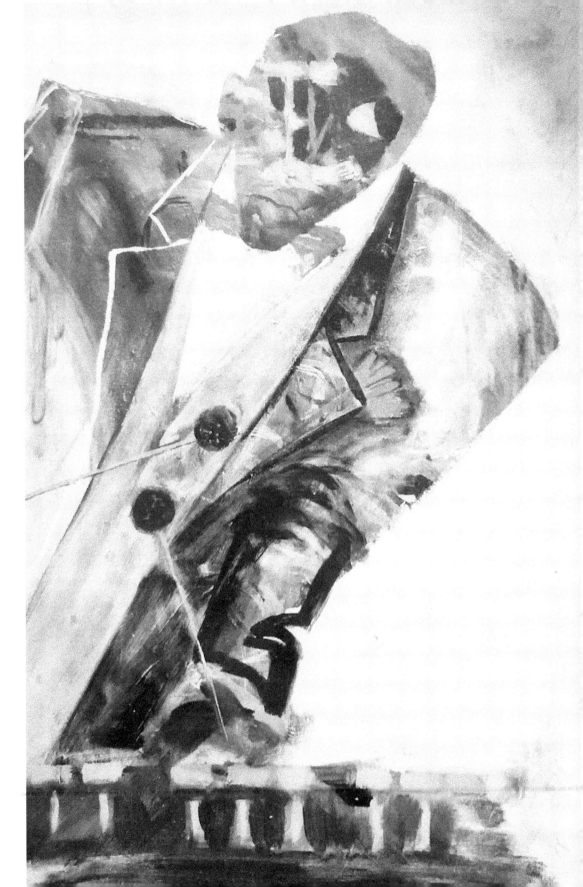

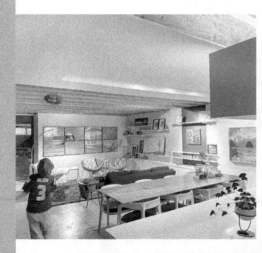

ROBERT ZIMMER AIA
ZIMMERRAYSTUDIOS / SEATTLE
LAS VEGAS / ZIMMERRAY.COM

JUDITH
SKILLMAN

Long Marriage Prayer
October's Mole
The Invalid
A July of July's

long marriage prayer

The lichen and the lichen's kin.
Rabbits black and black and white

sun themselves on winter days.
The dirt road leads to a tenement

where a man and a woman live
to peel back the skin of one

another until inside the core
the self's cut loose to fester and burn.

Do onion tears sting? The lichen
gray on green, the evening lengthening.

I wish for a crust of armor,
for stars on snow. I want

to hear the tinkle of snowmelt
and know that you left first.

OCTOBER'S MOLE

At it again, undoing the earth,
throwing cakes of dirt
up into light and rain,
shoveling through Hades.

Swimming the crawl stroke,
tunneling for the sake
of mystery into avenues
fragrant with worm-flesh

and feathered roots.
Infiltrating the myths,
ragged-toothed as an old woman
I called grandmother,

her hair half gone,
her voice a whisper.
At it like an intimate,
one who knows which song

makes me fall apart
and sings it just the same.
How masculine,
this rodent, no shovel,

no gloves, naked
except for the gray fur.
Undoing what was done.
In no hurry to remedy

wrongs, instead moving
on, carving out
more territory for the sake
of a secret wish.

THE INVALID

I come to her in the evening
when the earth has cooled
and gracious plants bow their heads
to the grass.

Her face a doppelganger,
her terrors born of fever dreams.
I make her comfortable
in the room of my childhood,

a barracks for the soldiers
of two world wars.
We sleep in one bed,
like Irish twins.

I crush an aspirin between spoons
and add sugar and juice.
When I stand
at the edges of her disappearance.

the room has a taste,
though it's been papered
with a skin of new wallpaper.
Japanese pagodas and whisper-flowers.

Julio returns from the morgue,
his face gone white
from making the identification
of his niece. She was killed at nine

on her pink bicycle,
sucked under a truck
on a Montreal boulevard.
I come to her every September.

How long before these Siamese
are separated? Will her nails
be painted in the nacre
of a common shell?

a July of July's

Heat on glass, the shifting begins.
Houses rise to ten degrees
above air temperature,
doors swell in their frames.

War contains no people,
only images. Those who live
on browning earth,
landlocked, have nowhere to go.

Nomads bear no children.
Tots with big brown eyes
like deer—already sacrificed
on Agamemnon's altar.

Outside, inside
remain countries apart.
Fire burns in the heart,
blood boils. Pretend water

never existed except in the mouth
of the crocodile, the slots
of the sprinkler, the scream
of the kettle.

MELISSA NIÑO
On the Foreign Custom of Sending Postcards
An Essay on Survival

on the foreign custom of sending postcards

…we were taught in school.
First, I stopped by *la papelería*
and asked for: an ENVELOPE.
Upper left corner:
the sender.
Lower right corner:
the receiver.
But, to me, the receiver
meant nothing.
I was ignorant of what it is
to receive a letter.
Until one of my aunties
emigrated to the United States.
Then I got not just letters
but stationary with matching envelopes
that weren't enough:
for I never got used
to sending postcards.
And yet, I do understand
when Wendell Berry talks
about Mattise's *Dominique*—
a presence in the light
stands in my window
like the silence of all those envelopes
I never used,
all destiny's orphans.

an essay on survival

It's true, sometimes the accumulation
of work and the commute become so thick
that one barely manages to hold the steering wheel,
but it's also true that indigence
makes light brighter
and when you least expect it, your skin
        softens
like the plshhhh of the green velvet
        campanula
crushed by the weight of a misstep
that returns you to reality

plshh plshh plshh plshh
¡corran, morros pendejos!
My fist firm and clenched
eyes half-closed that fix
their target in the distance,
all the prehistoric eternity of Eras
condensed in a second of immobility
just waiting to be free

because sometimes things ain't what they seem
and what we took as an ordinary scene
of kids in a crazy haze to get
the last chocobanana
is really

a girl holding a *slingshot*
her ammunition stockpile miscarried flowers
        picked from the soil
that she will use to gain advantage,
a woman holding a weapon (in her hand)
a woman hunting

it ain't a game though it is
and you are a filthy little girl that would rather not shower
because your mother, though tired, scrubs you
with the same conviction she puts into
scrubbing the *cochambre* off the damaged skillets
while all along the breeze passes,
because in order to say it enters
we first need a closed space
and the bathroom, involuntarily eco-friendly,
only has three walls, but no door

that's why we shall say the salty breeze of the Pacific
        passes
leaving you with goosebumps
and telling your mother it's time to stop
for no matter how hard she scrubs
you will keep being *morena*
in this land
where that color doesn't exist
it's called café and it's more similar to the surface
of the galeana tress carpeting the hellish asbestos ceiling
        in the bathroom,
'cause in this land of memory
that substance isn't forbidden yet
y 'cause north migrates to the south
and vice versa;

it's not me who says so but the whole
postcolonial studies school
I know because it´s what I've read at dawn
when the cold passes
leaving me with goosebumps
and indicating that it is time to return the books
to their cart

to organize the numbers backwards
from where I am now to the farthest
from history and geography to the zero point
from the yellow, inheritance of nicotine,
to the yellow of the flower buds
I burst as a child
from the warm yellow of the reading room
to the aseptic white of the cleaning room
and all the shelves in my charge

those of the chlorine, detergents, oils
and other high-end chemicals,
that do not cause irritation or have any aroma
and are bought in bulk
to reduce the ecological footprint *of the institution*
—but not that of my hands,
For that's
permanent,
it stores rainwater and dew
that attracts birds
during my meal time.

TRAVELING SOUL

KARI VAMARO

He is 91 years old. He wants to travel all around the world. Again. Kathy, his wife, is 90 years old. She tells him no. She takes his enormous hand tenderly in hers: We are too old to do something like that. We can barely move. You use a cane to walk. We can't drive. We cannot hear or even see very well. You need your nap. We are just too old.

He swims into her maritime eyes and for a little while he forgets everything. But just for a little while. Then he remembers. He wants to travel all around the world. Again. He thinks it is unfair his body has been a traitor to his traveling soul. He rejects her reasons. He knows she wants to travel too, but she is too well-advised.

They were wildly happy and had too much fun when they were travelers. Not as tourists. They were not taking pictures, being noisy, drinking too much and getting red. They enjoyed walking around the old towns in some unknown and unpronounceable country. They especially loved to walk into the small cemeteries, read the epitaphs, even if they did not understand the foreign metaphors, to leave some flowers. They looked for spots where they could drink several cups of hot black coffee, talking and watching how life goes on.

He finds a picture from those years. She is smiling to the camera with a small cemetery behind her and he is looking at her.

As usual. He is diving in her smile. She is taking his hand tenderly. As usual. They never lost that habit, nor the habit to drink black coffee together, even when doctors forbade it. But they did lose their habit to travel to a foreign place, to learn words from there. How many languages did they learn in those days? How many miles did they walk, in sync? How many prayers did they sing, and over how many graves? He wants to resume these habits.

So one night, while Kathy talks on the phone with their daughter Ashley, he packs a small suitcase for each, hiding them in the guest bathroom. He will surprise her tomorrow when she wakes. He'll ask her to take him to see the doctor. They will go by taxi because none of their daughters will know, but the taxi driver will. They will arrive at the airport, buying tickets for any flight that takes them to the capital of an exotic country.

The smile won't leave his face from glee. Kathy will be convinced when they are at the airport. He is certain of it. He falls asleep delighted for their new journey,

The next morning, Kathy discovers he has departed, this time without her, this time without a suitcase in towe, this time into light.

KEVIN MILLER

vanish

whispers its swish of sound
as a trail of breath follows
an image you hold like the title
of the film you saw two nights
ago, no longer on the tip of anything,
no aftertaste, no crumbs to help
find your way back to a place
you forget being, this little tremor
of fear when the ripples left
by the stone fail to reach the edge,
and the pond is a space as dark
as swallows you remember returning
to the nook above the door
in the garage behind the house
you find only in your sleep.

SCOTT RUESCHER

Above the Fold
Tag
At Hamilton and Pearl
Tenskwatawa

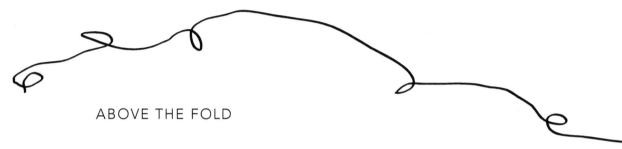

ABOVE THE FOLD

Halfway between the dates of the Kent State shootings
And my high school graduation, in late December of 1970,
I was home on Christmas vacation, kind of looking forward
To getting stoned alone in my basement bedroom, then smashed
At some New Year's Eve celebration with friends
While their parents were away, but was sitting down for lunch first
To skim the pages of the Columbus Dispatch, over a bowl
Of leftover spaghetti that I had sprinkled with parmesan
Shaken from a green Kraft cylinder, when I saw the bold caps
Of the frontpage headline from three hours south, 38 MINERS KILLED
IN COALMINE EXPLOSION, in a blast, added the sub-header caption,
That buried them instantly in the shaft of the Finley mine
At Hurricane Creek, just outside of Hyden, Kentucky,
When a stray electrical spark from a cutter, a planer, or a hammer,
The sort of machine that the men in my family made
On sheet-metal lathes at the Jeffrey Manufacturing company
Near downtown Columbus, ignited a cloud of coal dust gases—a blast
That asphyxiated and incinerated the four young men

SCOTT RUESCHER won the 2016 Write Prize from Able Muse, the 2015 Rebecca Lard Award from Poetry Quarterly, and, in both 2013 and 2014, the Erika Mumford Award for poetry about travel and international culture from the New England Poetry Club. His chapbooks include *Sidewalk Tectonics* (documenting a road-trip from Lincoln's birthplace in Hodgenville, Kentucky, to the site of ML King's assassination in Memphis) and *Perfect Memory* (documenting more of that same trip as well as adventures in such places as Central Ohio, Central America, and Central Square, Cambridge). For 15 years he has been administering the Arts in Education program at the Harvard Graduate School of Education and teaching part-time in the Boston University Prison Education Program—all while feeling vaguely skeptical about such intimate participation in institutions of higher learning.

In the full-color photograph below that who leaned my way

In clodhoppers and blue denim jackets, squinting for the camera

In the red autumn sunshine, big hearty boyish smiles

In their coal-blackened faces, mops of happy hair fringing

Their golden helmets, their names in the caption below the picture

A permutation of those I've since read on a monument in person,

Maybe Alonzo Couch, Kermit Hubbard, Teddy Bush, and Delbert

Henson, perhaps Grover Bowling, Walter Hibbard, Rufus Jones,

And Theo Griffin, or Decker Whitehead, Arnold Sizemore, Lawrence Gray,

And Denver Young, embodiments of a rambunctious male

American culture more than they were the pathological expressions

Of incestuous genealogies that northerners like to know them for,

Gathered after work one day for a Polaroid in front of the company store,

With a gravel road in the upper right corner curving away

Into a dark holler, joined at the shoulder in symmetrical order

Like carbon molecules in a covalent bond that has to endure

Constant pressure for millions of mineral years before

It can even begin to think about turning into diamonds.

TAG

Done giving directions in a textbook Spanish that the tourists
          Could understand, done closing out the register
Of pesos devalued to the equivalent of our dimes, and done
          Stocking the towering racks with dictionaries, maps,
And picture-postcard views of the monogamous volcanoes
          Of Mesoamerican myth that we had seen from certain
Perspectives in town — smoking-hot snow-cone Popo
          And his jagged wife Itzy — the pretty young women
Who ran the information booth in the town of Tlaxcala
          Were rolling down the corrugated blinds, turning off the lights,
Blowing each other their *buenas noches* kisses, and going their ways
          Down the narrow colonial avenues radiating from the fountain
In the hub of the *zócalo* like the spokes of a wheel —

          The one with glasses, we just knew, to join her family
For guacamole, quesadillas, refritos, and menudo
          In the kitchen of an apartment connected to the tortilla shop
That they'd named for Juan Diego, the 16th century Aztec man
          Who envisioned the Virgin Mary as an indigenous woman;
The one with the limp to the market pavilion beside the canal
          At the foot of the hill, where her parents sold tropical fruit —
Bananas, papayas, and mangos — from table-top pyramids modeled
          After those at Teotihuacan, the complex that resembles most

The Pentagon, in an aisle as long as *la Calle de los Muertos*,
Where fried grasshopper and *chicharrone* pork rind
Both can be found; and the one with long legs, crossing that canal
On a stone bridge and climbing the hill to the grade school
In the basement of the church we'd seen on the cliff from below,
To pick up her sister after work like she does every day —

To go straight up the hill, along the cactus fences guarding
The small garden plots of the pastel houses, where vines
Of magenta bougainvillea braid all the drainpipes,
Below the barking mongrels patrolling all the patios;
To take a right, just past the last house, at the crest of the hill,
And walk between cornfields in a cobblestone lane
To the church on the cliff, where a graveyard comes into view;
To see a line of little girls begin to meander toward her
From the cliff when they see her; to see them suspend
Their game of tag to admire her up close, visible only as black
Silhouettes against the sky at first; but to see them emerge,
Their black tresses streaming behind them like flags,
Their summer dresses white against their reddish-brown complexions,
From the aisles of the graveyard to gather in a line
Along the wall of the cemetery to greet her, the older sister
Of the beautiful little fleet-footed girl who was "it" until
Catching up with her classmates at the wall; and to let her look
Of big sisterly apprehension curl at both ends of her lips
Into a smile of recognition that also shifts her hips.

AT HAMILTON AND PEARL

Outdoors in shorts and tank top all summer, Henry hoed the rows
Of his plum tomato garden. He loosened the soil at the base
Of each plant. He watered around the roots before the sun had a chance
To swing around south. He served the plants manure tea
And mulched them with fertilizer from his compost heap.
We saw him from the kitchen window during breakfast on weekends,
Elbows and knees bent to the task, a warm white octogenarian
Sun-ripened Italian man, retired since the Seventies or so,
Who gardened, he said, "because it keeps me on my toes."
He had ears like snail shells and a nose like a hyacinth bulb,
Legs like knobby carrots, arms like parsnips, and a pension from a firm
That he tallied credits and debits for—and lived, we supposed,
On the meals his sister, Margaret, prepared for him upstairs,
In the second-floor apartment of the two-story yellow house
At Hamilton and Pearl. He liked chicken, salad, and pasta sauced
With his own plum tomatoes and homegrown garlic and basil.
Sometimes we saw him handing over bouquets of cultivated flowers
To the girls, old and young, who passed in seed and blossom
On the sidewalk of our thoroughfare—peonies and dahlias, acacias
And mums—with shy smiles, extended arms, and friendly phrases

Broccoli

Of everyday wisdom, formalities as familiar as the sunlight of summer.
It was none of our business, really, what Henry had been doing
For love for all those years. Was he a confirmed straight bachelor
Who couldn't be bothered, or a magna cum laude alumnus
Of the old school of queers? All we knew for certain was
That he marked the seasons with the blooming of his flowers,
From daffodil, crocus, and tulip, to lily, iris, and peony.
He was decisive in speech and action, self-reliant and independent,
And seemed to value intuition and reason in equal measure,
Buzzing around the garden like a bee all morning
With his watering can in hand, and his spade and claw in a bucket.
Sooner or later his roses bloomed too, and then Henry handed them,
All the way opened, to the beautiful neighbor women
He sometimes even knew by name. Those that remained,
When his girls had gone in to supper, he scattered along the prim hedge
Of the privet hedge he'd groomed with his pair of sharpened sheers,
If not with a pair of scissors, along the sidewalk in front.
By November, when the hedge's prickly foliage at the edges
Curled and fell, we saw the bare aluminum wires of the fence
For what they were—cautions not to invade the privacy
Of a man who'd rather deadhead petunias and talk about the weather.

TENSKWATAWA

Having, at the time, absolutely no career ambition
To be a doctor, an architect, a teacher, a politician,
Or a law-practicing poet who makes sociological connections
To his personal experiences, I paid less attention
To the Ohio history teacher's straightforward presentation
On the manifest destination of the colonial armies
Infiltrating Indian land in the Northwest Territories
From their forts along the "good river" of the Seneca people,
At confluences with the Miami, the Wabash, and the Muskingum,
    Than I did to the sight of Eddie, the charismatic custodian,
      Passing in the hallway with his bucket and his mop.
     I was more interested in staring at the spring warblers
    Picking hungry caterpillars from the crabapple blossoms
   Outside the classroom window, and at the snugly crossed legs
    Of my beautiful classmate Karen across the aisle from me.
    I didn't yet know that the story he told us the week before
     About the runaway slave, Eliza, in Uncle Tom's Cabin
      Crossing the Ohio on an ice floe with her baby,
Would mean as much to me one day, when I became completely
Obsessed with history, as a tributary that feeds the Ohio
Near the southernmost point in the whole state does
To the flow of the river—that the drainage water
From Eagle and Redoak Creeks would make its way, eventually,
From their confluence in Ripley to the muddy Mississippi.
I didn't yet wonder whether the runaways followed
Either of those minor creeks north from the hilltop home

Of abolitionist preacher John Rankin, now a small
Tourist attraction, to the popular route along the Scioto
And up through Columbus along Alum Creek and points north.
But I perked up and listened with an uncharacteristic fascination
that surprised everyone, myself included, when Mr. King,
Who also coached the football team, mentioned Tenskwatawa,

        A figure he said we should emulate for his altruistic
        Devotion to Tecumseh, his much more famous brother.
        I didn't know what it was about him—Tenskwatawa,
        The Shawnee medicine man we'd read about for homework
        In the textbook, also known as The Prophet, a visionary
        Who predicted the two earthquakes, in 1811 and 1812,
        That radiated from their epicenter in New Madrid, Missouri,
        On the western bank of the Mississippi; the loyal sibling
        Who sat by his brother at the Battle of the Thames
        In October of 1813, in an Ontario then still known
As Upper Canada, as he lay dying—when really it was Tecumseh
Who everyone was supposed to get all excited about
For trying to lead the indigenous nations, in confederacy
With the British, against the incursions of the colonists,
But who failed to unite the divided tribes of the East
And got so disheartened by that and by the defeat
To William Henry Harrison at the Battle of Tippecanoe,
And by the broken treaty with Mad Anthony Wayne, too,
That he led his diehard followers from the Greenville camp
In southwestern Ohio to the Battle of Fallen Timbers

        Up near Toledo, and finally on to Ontario, only
        To be ambushed in battle, to be shot right in the heart
        By a white man with a rifle, and to die in his brother's arms
        Inside a makeshift wigwam of poplar saplings and deer hides.

EILEEN WALSH DUNCAN

Cleaning the E.R.
Chimney Rock, Colorado
Cat's Tongue Fungus
Cantaloupe

CLEANING THE E.R.

How I learned to string fish in the Alaskan summer light,
threading line through heaving gills,
letting the length of flesh flip along the riverbank until dusk.
But now I am strung, a plastic hose up my sinus,
plunged down my esophagus, that sips CAT scan fluid
up from my stomach. Adrenalin floats me above the pain.

I quiver on the gurney, waiting.
I could be rolled down any hall, served up
to any masked group.
The curtains barely move as she glides in and nods.
She says, *I come to clean.*

My glassy eyes roll back, flashing yellowed sclera.
The room rolls with them. *Thank you,* I say.

The squick of the spray bottle, the stroke of wet paper
on laminate. Her thick belt hung
with packs of paper wipes. She rubs away
invisible swarms of germs as her gloves, a bit
too long for her fingers, bubble at the ends.

When I breathe slowly, I stop choking on the tube.
My hand finds the gurney edge and grips its coolness.
CT fluid and vomit are smattered on the floor.
How it glows, what was in me, that lit up
my shredded organ, and is now ejected
from that lightless place within.
I am sorry, I say, as she bends to it.

CHIMNEY ROCK, COLORADO
Elevation 7,867 feet

Our skins are a thin membrane
pulled and congealed
by our fleshy grip,
our small bones floating within.

We cling in the weightless air,
blotting the rocks in a porous ascent
along the sharp summit edge.

Gravity shimmers and rolls down
like beaded mercury.

But here: the tendril prints
of ancient seas, a shrimp
sunk into silt,

its briny limbs sifting sand,
now sleeping the blank sleep
of rock, infinity's repose.

Light pours along raven's back,
enamored.

We are not shaped of bedrock
or feathery sandstone,
but of water and lucent tissue,
a soup that stirs its restless self.

We sit. We close our eyes
and spiral up among the peregrines
who ascend too high,
and press moth-quick wings to the sun.

They return, their cries quiver
along our bodies
and the bald rock.
We feel for a moment
what it is to go beyond.

cat's tongue fungus

If decaying logs and stumps wished to speak,

would they choose this manner of tongue:

translucent, gelatinous, emergent in clusters?

And could each smooth-capped arc, with its spiny

underside, say enough of the endless swells of wind,

the ache of lifting water drop by drop from aquifers?

A tree's slow descent into earth can take decades,

as did its rise. Tiny things run through the paths

where sapwood was once bound by growth rings:

the chewers, the diggers, miniature jaws and claws

do this meticulous work, the dismemberment.

As shards and wisps come loose and drift,

form siftable mounds on the soil surface,

these fungi nudge out of what remains cohered,

emanating light from nowhere. A tree, of all beings,

would glide like this, speak only in sprout and glow

on its journey to rejoin the particulate.

cantaloupe

Grip the lacy exoskeleton, feel the heft
pull along forearm and bicep. Its hollow head
     is always heavier than expected.
Nor would you guess the inner landscape,
     the sea of sweet held by tinted tissue,
     the slope of seeds tucked, strung
along darker cords, umbilical, somnolent.
     Last of all would you imagine the air,
     aspirated in tiny blips under the passing
     of sun, of moon. For months
     the orbs swell and whorl,
deliberate in their movement. This secret air
     is the heart of a melon; flesh grows
away from it. I wonder what becomes
of it as I slice and prise the sucrose brawn
     from its weightless,
     invisible core.

EILEEN WALSH DUNCAN'S work has been nominated for a Pushcart Prize.
She lives in the Pacific Northwest under innumerable Douglas firs.

ALLISON PAUL

I am a Sequoia
Sometimes I Chop Onions
Lessons from Trees

I am sequoia

> "...fire, the great destroyer of Sequoia, also furnishes bare virgin
> ground, one of the conditions essential for its growth from
> the seed." - John Muir, *The Mountains of California,* 1894

Sequoia trees must burn to survive.

Fire blazes the way for seedlings, removing bark beetle infested

individuals and leaf litter kindling on the forest floor,

breaking down before rebuilding,

to protect the ecological balance of the forest.

Yes, some saplings are sacrificed for the good of the grove.

The upside down V,

blackened and indented

on the bark of mature trees,

a cave, a shelter,

a tattoo marking resilience,

it's furrows becoming more prominent, a now wise tree,

stronger for the V.

It withstood.

It stood.

I am sequoia

"...fire, the great destroyer of Sequoia, also furnishes bare virgin
ground, one of the conditions essential for its growth from
the seed." - John Muir, *The Mountains of California*, 1894

I burn to survive.

Fire blazes the way

for my seedlings,

removing bark beetle infested individuals and leaf litter kindling,

breaking down before rebuilding to protect our ecological balance.

Yes, some saplings are sacrificed for the good of the grove.

The upside down V,

blackened and indented

on my bark,

a cave, a shelter,

a tattoo marking the struggle and triumph.

My furrows became prominent, now a wise tree,

stronger for the V.

I withstood

and still I stand.

lessons from trees

Tell me, Reader,

how do you reconcile

the duality of immortality and finitude?

Adopt a cedar mentality –

healer and protector.

Build fences around your saplings, but put a gate in.

Pay attention to your roots. They store blueprints

to reference as you adapt to a shifting environment.

Your journey is a juniper,

Reader. Let your bark spiral

and bend as you discover

the perennial nature of existence.

Become a larch and shed your adornment when it be-

comes gilded. Welcome winter and know you are not the

only one

with deciduous qualities.

sometimes I chop onions

I find myself inundated
with news of tragedy and hatred.
I used to cry,
but eventually the tears got stuck
and have since become backlogged grief.
Like truckers in a traffic jam after a heavy snow, they turned off their
engines
in the middle of the deserted highway
and waited.
They thought it would only last a few hours, but after the seventh day
they emitted noxious impatience.
They played cruel games,
like Peptic Ulcer Relay Race
and Berate the Insurance Representative,
any way to ignore the enormous pool of magma welling up in their
chests, threatening to squeeze pain through the arterial route
and erupt in public.
All they want
is to resume their delivery route, exit the highway,
and be welcomed by their families.
That blockade miles ahead isn't budging,
so I devised an unconventional escape route.

CLAUDIA CASTRO LUNA IS WASHINGTON'S STATE POET LAUREATE (2018 – 2021) and served as Seattle's inaugural Civic Poet (2015-2017). She is the recipient of an Academy of American Poets, Poets Laureate Fellowship and the author of *Killing Marías* (Two Sylvias) finalist for the WA State Book Award 2018, *This City* (Floating Bridge) and *One River, a Thousand Voices* (Chin Music Press) Born in El Salvador she came to the United States in 1981. *https://wapoetlaureate.org/poetry-to-lean-on/* ***POEMS TO LEAN ON: FOR SOLACE, RESILIENCE, HOPE*** *Submit at poet@humanities.org*

morning star

Along the way

you do things

you don't want to do,

things, you know

you should not do,

things you don't know

how to stop doing.

No one can see beyond

the wave's crest.

Then you find yourself

sitting there, wherever you are

blemished and imperfect.

That is life. This carrying on

of our dented selves

alongside the spoonful of sugar

we also carry within.

A sweet grain

for each good, right thing

we too have done

along the way.

by
CLAUDIA CASTRO LUNA

GHOST TROUT

RUSSELL HILL

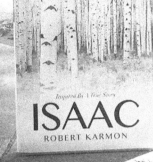

Inspired By A True Story

ISAAC

ROBERT KARMON

THE FABRICATIONS
THE FABRICATIONS
THE FABRICATIONS

Goodbye to
Tenth Street

A novel
by Irving Sandler

The Law of the Unforeseen

Poems by
Edward Harkness

TWILIGHT in Danzig

A novel by
SIEGFRIED KRA

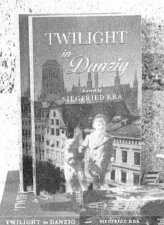

TWILIGHT in DANZIG   SIEGFRIED KRA
TWILIGHT in DANZIG   SIEGFRIED KRA
TWILIGHT in DANZIG   SIEGFRIED KRA

50% off
ALL BACKLISTED
T I T L E S

C O D E :

IF YOU
MAY
PLEASE
BUY
YOUR
PLEASURE
B O A T
BOOKS
DIRECT-
LY FROM
PLEASURE
BOAT
Studio
.COM TO
H E L P
SUPPORT
T H I S
LITTLE
P R E S S
AND ITS
AUTHORS.
IT'S JUST
A B O U T
THE ONLY
WAY TO
MAKE A
DIME IN
THIS BIZ.

#survivalkits

a few of the brilliant books hidden inside these vague covers. check them out and more at *pleasure boat studio .com*

FREE SHIPPING ON ALL BOOKS, OLD OR NEW

& please let us know what you think of old and especially new releases on Amazon or Goodreads. If you do it for any book, send me the link and I'll send you a free backlisted title of you choice, if we have it in stock! thanks so much for your support!

bookclubs 30% off

C O D E :

BOOKCLUB

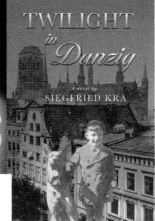

Goodbye to Tenth Street

RUSSELL HILL

NEWER RELEASES 2017 TO 2019
25% OFF. CODE: #STORYTIME

GHOST TROUT
by Russell Hill

"Like a canvas that is painted with precise strokes, this set of narrative moments freezes your attention on universal images." -Russell Chatham (writer and painter)

"Another marvelous collection, this one filled with tiny explosions of narration and exposition. A book you'll keep picking up to find something new that touches on your life." -Don Christians (KWMR FM radio)

"It's an extraordinary piece of writing. I know nothing about fly fishing. Many of the landscapes are unfamiliar to me (though a few I recognize). Yet I found myself deeply immersed and captivated and moved. The beauty of the language, its restraint, the deep and plainspoken thought—it's almost like a book length poem, or a kind of koan. The people spring to life in startlingly few words. The image of your dying neighbor and his single light bulb stubbornly burning will stay with me forever. I'm so glad [Hill] wrote it and so glad that I read it. I hope it finds its way into people's hands, because it deserves to be read." -Jesse Kellerman

"GHOST TROUT is a wonderful book. It is poetic, but better than that the book is honest and the voice is trustworthy." -Louis Phillips

From The New York Times / Roberta Smith NYT: The BEST ART BOOKS of 2018:

'GOODBYE TO TENTH STREET: A NOVEL' By Irving Sandler (Pleasure Boat Studio). Anyone drawn to the postwar art scene that centered on Manhattan's East 10th Street should read the last book of Mr. Sandler, the art historian and critic extraordinaire who died in June. He was there in the late 1950s and early '60s taking notes while the Abstract Expressionists made history, and he became known for his meticulous accounts of their saga. But here he offers a roman à clef filled with the unverified gossip, overheard conversations, and rumors of nooners and backbiting that were unsuitable to fact-based history (though a few historical figures occupy the margins). The tale -- from charged studio visits to nasty exchanges at the Cedar Bar -- has its own sad, sordid, unsurprising truth.

THE FABRICATIONS by
Baret Magarian

"Never more prescient than in our post-fact world—in which reality TV show figures who never read books but watch endless hours of television hold the highest political offices in the land, The Fabrications' satire is spot on...a tour de force of the literary imagination....It's a wondrous novel both cleverly satirical of our spectacle-based society and philosophically profound, a rare accomplishment." ~Lee Foust, The Florence News

"...Oscar Babel is a film projectionist and painter who's lost hope of finding success. Daniel [a bored mainstrteam writer] decides to write a story about the Oscar who could be, a man who lives to his fullest potential... he conceives of Oscar as a pop philosopher, worshipped by the masses and incapable of doing wrong. Soon, Oscar ends up in the clutches of Ryan Rees, a talent agent who intends to "take a complete nobody and turn him into a *prophet*."....Oscar's messianic ascent is entertaining (think Stravinsky's riotous 1913 work *The Rite of Spring*)...A resplendent tale about an unlikely prophet that deserves to be pondered at length and acted on." -*Kirkus Reviews*

TWILIGHT IN DANZIG
By Siegfried Kra

"Dr. Kra's father owned a very prosperous coal business...Siegfriend knew only the very best of what life had to offer. [Soon] his German governess entered him in the Hitler youth [being told it was boy scouts]...The clouds of anti-Semitism were rapidly dimming the lives of the Kra family. The prelude to the Holocaust had begun. It is difficult for us today to understand the horrible events leading to the Holocaust, and the Holocaust itself. That is why narratives like Twilight in Danzig are so important, providing personal insight into these devastating and tragic events." -Reviewed by Editor Emeritus Michael M. Deren, MD, Ct Medicine Magazine

"This book provides a luscious and haunting account of a world that would be forever altered by the advent of World War 2. 1930's Danzig, now Gdansk, comes to life! The book takes the reader back to witness, as the young protagonist does, the quickly changing sense of normalcy and ever increasing danger before Hitler's invasion of Poland." -a reader

**SUPPORT
INDEPENDENT
BOOKSTORES
& PRESSES!**

Various photographs,
art, photoshopped
collages, collages made from
magazines, scissors and glue,
and layouts from iphone photographs; intro, last page, postscript writing & imagery by:

LAUREN GROSSKOPF, Native Seattleite, Publisher / book
designer for Pleasure Boat Studio: A Nonprofit Literary Press.
She lives in West Seattle, is a grateful mama to her awesome
nine year old, Maude, and occasionally makes other visual art
during her free time.

**I am available to design books & marketing materials,
but will no longer be receiving new submissions, due to
financial reasons. Thank you! Books will continue to be
sold on the online bookstore: pleasureboatstudio.com.**

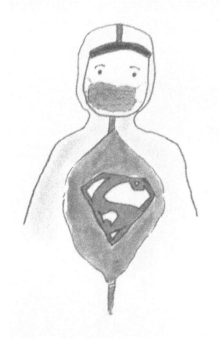

BY AYA WEBB, AGE 13,
Amsterdam. Artist, Sachi
Webb's daughter. For the
middle school zine.

BY MAUDE WELKER, AGE 9,
Refridgerator Batman art
still up from a few years ago. For
the elementary school zine.

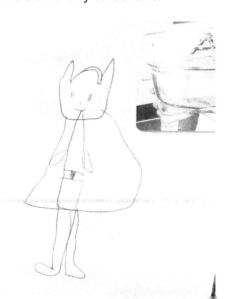

LIGHTS, is being released while people are largely quarantined, connecting remotely in a 'vira-cation' for some, while a gruesome life and death battle for others....Either way, we are all trying to escape a dangerous, invisible threat that could lurk anywhere and possibly put someone else's life or death in our unwitting hands. Stylish face masks have quickly flooded the streets.

I have also instigated a **'KIDS FOR KIDS' ZINE, *FOR KIDS BY KIDS,*** so people of all ages can have another outlet to connect in positive, creative ways. I imagine the experience could be lightening and refreshing, and kids will have a place on peoples's shelves to be honored as they are, by us and by each other.

The idea for making a KIDS FOR KIDS imprint came about when my daughter, Maude was little, because I really love adult-made kids' books; and I also really adore kid's creative expressions. They have their own heartwarmingly-imperfect, funny, ridiculous, cute, silly, bizarre, sometimes wildly out of control and touchingly sloppy styles...and when younger, from a place of unselfconscious acceptance and unique imaginations that think of things in far different ways than adults. I thought it would be fun for kids to read stories, comics, see art, photos of lego structures they made, jokes, etc *for kids by* kids. All in all, a zine is a creative-collective, and that's a good thing. And of course, the older folks would enjoy it too.

AMMENDMENT: With the continued pandemic and protests, it could also be therapeutic, as well as historical. It would be incredible if this became a thing, state to state, country to country and shared in libraries around the world, or a website for all to post. Some Themes they can work with: The pandemic, the protests, homeschooling, dreams for the future, and what we can do for the environment and to help people, and of course lights. Anything else, as long as it's positive, is welcome.

OPTIONAL TEMPLATES AVAILABLE: 7.10.20
in a PDF if people would like a little structure c/o
pleasureboatstudio.com.
ART DUE: 8.15.20 / ONLINE PDF: 9.15.20
Printed copies will also be available.
Send work to: Lauren@pleasureboatstudio.com

161

spot
stage
flash
candle
string of
reading
fire
star
lightning bug
moon
sun
head
back
lamp
city
cloud filtered
holiday
chandlier
cracked door
microscope
projector
key hole
pen
screen
switches
house
overhead
grungy
cool
florescent
car
stadium
sky
dawn's
dusk's
afternoon
eye
mind's
love's
lime
infrared
blue
black
red
all the color spectrum's rays of
aurora borealus
street
film
elegant
bright
warm
fresh
easy
pure
clean
sparkly
effervescant
mysterious
mood
low
blazing
fireworks
lifted
disco
scattered
misty
hazey
the lights within

lights give us a way to see in the dark,

they show us things

now you can see...

now you can see where you are

and where you're going

where we all could be going

spotlight on a stage

candle when the power's out

flashlight, chandelier, desklamp, moon,

city lights, star lights

fires to read by

to be still or active in the sun

if we can just learn from this,

to slow down, share the wealth,

not strive so hard that we break the world

and each other...

for a lighter, more cohesive

society, a cleaner environment and

less fractured, healthier future.

postscript

GEORGE
FLOYD
8 : 4 6
SILENCE
IS VIOLENCE

DAVID GROSSKOPF
June 8, 2020

Dear Derek Chauvin's knee,

You have been blamed for cutting off the air of George Floyd, of leaning on his neck while he begged for breath and his mother, and Derek Chauvin now stands accused of murder in the second degree. We are now entering the third week of growing protests to what your uninterrupted eight minutes and fortysix seconds mean in this country, the long minutes of "I can't breathe I can't breathe" ignored by Derek Chauvin and three officers who didn't stop you from Floyd's neck as bystanders said you're killing him you've probably killed him get off do something, a kneeling that would later call to mind Colin Kaepernick's knee protesting uninterrupted brutality of police that absurdly and eventually lost Kaepernick his job after the President said Get that son of a bitch off the field right now he's fired, and later, Derek Chauvin's knee, after you stopped George Floyd's breath, the President and his approving 42% angrily decried movement on the streets saying Why can't you protest peacefully, and the protesters say to the police but also to you, I can't breathe.

I learned about unarmed Michael Stewart being strangled by transit police who were acquitted of his absurd murder. I learned about unarmed Amadou Diallo who was caught in a hailstorm of 42 bullets by police acquitted of his absurd murder. I learned about woodcarver John Williams who was shot multiple times by police never charged with his absurd murder. I learned about unarmed teenager Trayvon Martin shot by neighborhood watch who was acquitted of his absurd murder. I learned about unarmed boy Tamir Rice who was shot playing in a playground by police who were cleared of his absurd murder. I learned about unarmed hands-up Michael Brown who was shot six times by police who was acquitted of his absurd murder. I learned about handcuffed Freddie Gray who died from a rough ride delivered by police who were acquitted of his absurd murder. I learned about armed but not reaching Philando Castile who was shot seven times by police who was acquitted of his absurd murder. I learned about unarmed Charleena Lyles shot in her apartment by the very police she called and who were then cleared of her absurd murder. I learned about unarmed Botham Jean who was shot in his apartment by police who at last was charged with his absurd murder. I learned about unarmed Breonna Taylor who was shot in her apartment by police in a no-knock midnight raid under current investigation. And I learned about unarmed Eric Garner who begged the same fucking thing we heard six years later from George Floyd when police didn't let up and killed him and who were never indicted for his absurd murder, even after he said, and George Floyd said, and thousands and thousands and thousands of African Americans on the streets begging for air said, I can't breathe.

That was you on George Floyd. That was my knee on America's neck, for far longer than eight minutes and forty six seconds, Black America gagging as I did and said nothing.

Police brutality, echos of Nazis...
DEFUND THE POLICE.
Allocate funds to help people.

'LIGHTS' CAME OUT PRIOR TO GEORGE FLOYD & THE GLOBAL PROTESTS, AT THE RISK OF AN UPTICK IN COVID CASES. THIS POSTSCRIPT IS FOR THE INCLUSION OF THIS HISTORICAL MOMENT, AS WELL AS BECAUSE SILENCE IS COMPLICIT.

Masked protestors appear as metaphor, that the citizens of the world can't / won't breathe this toxic air anymore. AWARE OF OUR BREATH, AS WE BREATHE LESS COMFORTABLY THROUGH MASKS, NO ONE HAS THE RIGHT TO TAKE OUR BREATH–OUR LIFE–AWAY. PROTESTING WITH MASKS, A SLIGHT VISCERAL REMINDER OF GEORGE FLOYD'S PLEAS FOR HIS OWN. The world-wide quarantine, brought on in large part by our destruction of forests, was the pause that jarred us out of our lives. Covid-19 stopped the noise of busy routines and made us take note of spikes ripping our canvas, spikes we weren't paying close enough attention to. Never again!

RACISM IS UNDENIABLY A PUBLIC HEALTH ISSUE
(APHA'S GEORGES BENJAMIN IN POPULAR SCIENCE)

At the end of the *The Two Popes*, during a montage of speeches around the globe, the new Pope says: "We become used to the suffering of others...I don't have anything to do with it.
It must be someone else. Certainly, not me.
When no one is to blame,
everyone is to blame."

My grandfather used to say,
"We are all equal. No one is above me, and I am above no one else."
My grandparents were Holocaust survivors from Poland.

My father was born at the end of the war, in Russia and spent his first five years in a displaced persons camp in Germany before taking a boat to America. His first language was Yiddish, and he had yet to learn English when he began attending a South Beach, Miami elementary school. He felt embarrassed to be dressed differently in European short pants and shoes. However, he wondered why everyone was speaking gibberish and didn't make sense, unlike himself. Yet, he couldn't be more proud to be an American. This sentiment is both sweet and sad. How proud can we be that this is our America? May our children and the following generations do better than we have. And yet, we can be proud of the positive movement and change, to know that most people want to work towards a more just, equal, accepting, healthier world.

I am dedicating this last section to my family. I didn't mean to, it just happened that way. My father and Aunt Donna Slotsky sometimes remind us of a principle of Judaism, **TIKKUN OLAM**, a Hebrew phrase that means **TO REPAIR THE WORLD**.

The other day, my Dad, Barry Grosskopf, said a feeling I have had as well before, however in different words, *"mother nature made this world so beautiful and gave us an appreciation for aesthetics, to give us some graciousness. Covid was like a slap from nature, [like flicking fleas off herself as he demonstrated], that if we don't do something, in 20-30-100 years, humidity could be at 90 percent, temps at 95—most of us can't survive that... [And] Trump was the catalyst for this, bringing out the ugliest of white supremacy that came out in full force with his backing. The police have been acting like a gang, by having each other's backs."*

Trump and his people are 'LIKE' a mafia family. Can we please have more liberals in positions of power forever? The polarism is exhausting and often progress-defeating. My parents and their friends were/are peace and equal rights activists. It's how I grew up.

I love this picture recently sent to me of my Mom, Myrna Grosskopf, later to come out as lesbian and became a public defender (1945-1990), flipping the bird. I'm giving this to the cops, to bigotry, to an unfair economic and justice system, to the white-supremacists, neo-nazis, to the billionaires not sharing their wealth, to our life and nature-threatening economy and medical system that is fueled by money before people, wildlife and the planet; and to the lack of massive policy reforms that have yet to be made, that would ensure the environmental protection absolutely necessary right now and for the future. For a few years, I thought it would take a revolution, pressure has been building from every angle of society and millions of people are on the same page. This is the beginning. We need a grand remodel! All the infrastructure and every room in the house. It's time for an upgrade.

My hand written protest-shirt against Lincoln Park's sky.

My daughter, Maude,
protesting & cheering for

BLACK LIVES MATTER

Feminist from day one, of her own accord, and a love for Martin Luther King, Jr.,
there is no doubt that we can continue the efforts to repair the world with heartfelt,
peaceful care, as she unintentionally is symbolizing here.

EXCERPT FROM:

SPEAK TO THE MOUNTAIN, THE TOMMY WAITES STORY
AS TOLD BY DR. BESSIE W. BLAKE,
PLEASUREBOATSTUDIO.COM

FROM THE INSIDE FLAP:
"Tommie's journey of endurance and ultimate victory over poverty, sickness, racism, sexism and the abusive relationship of an alcoholic husband, coupled with her stamina to sustain a vital ministry into the new millennium, is a testament to the resilience of the human spirit. Her story inspires the hopeless and strengthens the faithful as she reminds us to rise above our circumstances.... I am happy to endorse *Speak to the Mountain*.... Read this book. Your spirit will soar and you too will be encouraged to stand against the odds."
-from the Foreword by Gordon Parks

I imagine you know the story of the widow woman. It's in the eighteenth chapter of Luke starting at the first verse. You can go and read it for yourself, but I want to speak in plain English and make her story relevant to us today:

The widow woman went before an unjust judge and asked him to do something about her adversary. He was going to ignore her, but she persisted in going to him. We don't know if he was harsh in his tone with her. We do know, however, that he did not help her. She didn't give up though. She kept returning with her request: "I want you to do something about my adversary."

...

"Ma'am, what you waiting on?"

"Oh, the judge is going to avenge me of my adversary today."

"Well, you've been coming everyday and he hasn't done anything."

"Yeah, but he is going to do it today."

Sometimes, we have to get positive about what we want from the Lord. On her first trip to the judge, she might have said, "I came to see if he can avenge me." Next day, maybe it was, "I sure hope he can get to me today." However, that last day she came in with boldness, "The judge IS going to avenge me of my adversary today."

When we ask God for something, we are supposed to ask with a positive attitude...Finally the judge got tired of his aide coming in to report, "The little widow is back out there."

"You mean that woman came back? She's been here all these days? She must be crazy. Well, I will have to do something 'cause she's worrying me. She's getting on my nerves." She didn't care about getting on his nerves. All she wanted was justice.

More of us need to be like the widow woman: don't give up and don't let the devil upset us; all he has to work with is fear. We need to resist the devil and overcome the evil we encounter...

Some of us never would have gotten restitution because we would have been too busy getting the judge told. Not the little widow woman! She didn't mind being ignored. She waited confidently on the judge to do his job. We're too quick to throw up our hands but that woman was patient and persistent and that's what it is going to take for us. If we want to make heaven our home, we must be patient and persistent. Regardless to who gives up...a parable to this end, that men ought always to pray, and not to faint.

In other words, don't give up. Have faith.

Some of us might not relate to the prayer idea, but the message is potent from this ancestor of slaves, a foundational element to this country, after the annhilation of Native Americans, currently shaking its roots from old, hardenned ground. Periods of history bring fierce fights or revolution, but every step towards human rights is a step in the right direction.

BLACK LIVES MATTER